MY LIFE STAMP

As a youth with little a plan,
My dad oft asked,
"What footprints are you going to leave in the sand?"

It meant little then,
But with time,
This became a motivating line.

If up to me,
What will be,
My ultimate legacy?

A legacy for me,
It would seem,
A far off, lofty dream.

After all, who am I?
I'm just average,
Somewhat shy.

Then I realized something you see,
It is up to me,
My ultimate legacy.

Social media, search,
Mobile, and more,
Leave digital footprints on the floor.

Digital shadows,
If you will,
Following all that I fulfill.

My grandchildren and great grandchildren,
What will they see and think of me?
What is my digital ˡ

D1113881

Will they see that I pursued my dream,
Or that I settled,
For something in-between?

That I lived a life doing things I loved,
Or one filled with,
Should of, could of?

Digital footprints remain for all time,
So I can't commit,
The ultimate crime.

What is that crime, you say?
It is, of course,
Not seizing the day.

Yes, before I die,
I'd rather fail,
Than not even try,

I will reach for the sky,
Laugh,
And cry.

I'll cry from joy not sorrow,
Because I lived for today
And planned for tomorrow.

My legacy,
You see,
Is truly up to me.

That's my view,
But, now I ask,
What will you do?

Written by Erik Qualman from his book *Digital Leader*

· · · · ·

WHAT HAPPENS
≡ In ≡
VEGAS
STAYS ON → YOU TUBE

ERIK QUALMAN

EQUALMAN STUDIOS
Cambridge MA

For my beautiful wife and daughters.

You make the world a better place.

● ● ● ● ●

WHAT HAPPENS IN VEGAS STAYS ON YOUTUBE
Equalman Studios
Cambridge, MA
www.equalman.com

Cover design by Dan Dinsmore
Interior design by Erin Stark for TLC Graphics, www.TLCGraphics.com

ISBN: 978-0-9911835-0-0

Printed In the United States of America

• • • • •

**"We don't have a choice on whether
we do social & mobile, the choice
is in how well we do it."**

• • • • •

The above quote seems illogical. After all, do I not have a choice regarding my use of social and mobile outlets or any new technology? Would avoidance of these new tools protect my reputation?

You could choose the path of technology avoidance, but it would be increasingly difficult to succeed without these digital tools and your reputation could still be compromised. Regardless if you elect to use social media or have a digital presence, people will be looking for you online. When you do not create and manage your digital reputation, you allow others to do this for you. Would you rather have influence over your reputation, or give that control to others?

For example, research indicates that 92% of children under the age of two already have a digital posting about them.[i] Yes, what happens offline stays online. This is a fundamental shift in society. It is a shift that many of us, from schoolteachers to CEOs, have failed to grasp. By reading this book, you have made the choice to produce and protect your best reputation. Nice choice.

TABLE OF CONTENTS

PREFACE

If connecting and communicating with students is at the heart of our work, social media is no longer an addition to our work... it is our work. Social networking sites like Twitter, Instagram and Facebook have become primary venues for traditional college-aged students to connect and communicate information. A 2013 Pew Research Center report shows 90% of young adults (age 18-29) are using social networking sites. Further, the 2013 EDUCAUSE Center for Analysis and Research study shows that technology enhances student engagement by facilitating connections to peers, instructors, and the institution. Certainly, while student engagement literature, for the most part, has focused on face-to-face interactions, Student Affairs educators need to adopt a new mindset to effectively meet the needs of 21st century students. Social media in higher education has created opportunities for discourse and exploration in a time when new perspectives must be considered. This is where Student Affairs educators can play an important role.

From new student orientation and leadership development to career services and residential education, the student affairs field is uniquely positioned to educate students as to the benefits and challenges of maintaining a positive online reputation. Lessons of civility, ethics, communication, and wellness that have historically fit within the traditional student affairs model must now be translated to an online realm. As educators, it is our obligation to move beyond cursory social media knowledge and model smart online behavior.

It's no secret that digital technology has become a valued and desirable skill in the modern workplace. The National Association of College Employers (NACE) 2014 job outlook report identifies the top skills and qualities employers seek in graduates including the ability to:

- Verbally communicate with persons in and outside the organization
- Work in a team structure
- Make decisions and solve problems
- Plan, organize, and prioritize work
- Obtain and process information
- Analyze quantitative data
- Apply technical knowledge related to the job
- Develop proficiency with computer software programs
- Create and/or edit written reports
- Sell or influence others

Integrating social media into a 21st Student Affairs pedagogy can enhance and develop these important competencies. This book is an ideal starting point for aspiring undergraduate leaders; graduate students in higher education preparatory programs; professionals seeking guidance and best practice advice; and an excellent focus for a senior academic or administrative colloquium. *What Happens in Vegas Stays on YouTube* is filled with valuable lessons, relevant examples, timely humor, and rich multimedia resources that will assist everyone in creating and maintaining a proud and powerful digital legacy.

This book is just one of many exciting new initiatives for the newly formed "Digital Technology in Student Affairs Practice" task force at ACPA–College Student Educators International. This comes on the heels of rapid change and paradigm shifting ideas that took place at this past year's international convention in Indianapolis, Indiana. In the coming months, we'll unveil an all-star cast of scholars, practitioners, and researchers that will look to continue that momentum. We invite YOU to join the conversation as together we explore exciting new questions, possibilities, and challenges that impact our students and professionals in this fast-paced, technological world.

Many thanks to Heather Shea-Gasser, Kathleen Kerr, Paul Gordon Brown, Tricia Fechter, Kent Porterfield, Cindi Love, and Gavin Henning for their progressive leadership and support in advancing ACPA's role as a higher education leader in the digital, connected age.

Ed Cabellon and Tony Doody
Co-Chairs of ACPA's Presidential Task Force
on Digital Technology

INTRODUCTION

Privacy is dead. Reputations are dying. Do not let it happen to your company, your team or your family. You need to turn this potential liability into leadership, and you need to start today. Learn the art and science behind why digital reputations are determining:

- Business winners and losers
- Your child's future
- Effective vs. ineffective CEOs & school teachers
- Your team's culture
- Church congregation sizes
- Your next job
- Everything...

Whether you are a schoolteacher, senator, CEO, soccer mom, coach or pastor, you must understand the new rules of today's transparent society and pass this book onto your employees, kids, boss, players and congregation.

This book can be read in a day, but referenced for a lifetime. Everyone important to you deserves this gift. Its 36 essential rules ensure you produce and *preserve your most important asset — your reputation*.

It's not just about surviving; it's about thriving and being:

- Industry Leaders vs. Industry Followers
- Hired vs. Fired
- Promoted vs. Demoted

- Winners vs. Losers
- Inspired vs. Tired
- FLAWsome

Instead of shame, these tips will help you and your organization achieve the fame you so richly deserve. The explosion of mobile and social technologies means that we have to live as if our mother, boss, coach and enemies are watching us... because they are. Success is a choice in this digital age, but we only have this choice if we understand the new rules.

Why 36 rules? Because there are 36 numbers on a roulette table and if you do not understand these rules then you are truly playing Russian roulette with your future.

It's not a question of *if* you will make a mistake, it's a question of *when* and *how* you will *capitalize* on turning digital lemons into digital lemonade. Learn to be FLAWsome.

Whether it's business or personal, your digital reputation *is* your reputation.

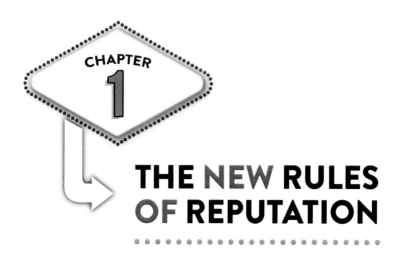

THE NEW RULES OF REPUTATION

1. Common sense is not that common
2. Live as though your mother is watching
3. KISS: Keep It Super Simple
4. 100% LinkedIn profile completion
5. Don't post whispers
6. Integrity & reputation are now one
7. What's your digital compass?
8. Be "FLAWsome"
9. Privacy is your problem
10. Have one digital identity
11. Complain = Digital Pain
12. Post it forward
13. Network before you need your network
14. Praise publicly, criticize privately
15. Words: Measure twice, post once
16. The three-second rule
17. We will make digital mistakes—how we handle them defines us

18. Multitasking = Mistakes

19. Be trustworthy

20. It's not the crime, but the cover-up

21. Make ginormous public goals

22. Face-2-Face cannot be replaced

23. Tinderbox Topics—Caution!

24. The power of a letter

25. Cyberbullying: Don't enable it

26. See your kids as others see them

27. Be authentic

28. Fail fast, fail forward, fail better

29. Freedom of choice — Not freedom from consequence

30. Adhere to the Golden Rule

31. You represent your company, organization & family

32. Be a Baker not an Eater

33. Your Legacy = Digital Footprints + Digital Shadows

34. Surround yourself with success

35. Watch your language

36. Teach & train your team, employees & family

• • • • •

"A man is the sum of his actions,
of what he has done,
of what he can do, nothing else."

GANDHI

• • • • •

No. 1

Common Sense is Not That Common

- Smart people make costly gaffes by posting items digitally without using common sense or by committing inappropriate acts offline that are posted online by a witness.

- The new reputation rules in this book will help you increase your digital common sense and avoid public digital blunders. These easy to remember concepts will not only help you survive, but also thrive in this digital age. You will present and protect your best self.

- Already have digital common sense? Gift this book to a person you care about who is not so savvy (e.g., co-worker, employee, teammate, spouse, son). For a refresher, I encourage you to review these rules occasionally as well.

- When it comes to your digital reputation, it is always best to have command of your destiny. In today's world, your digital reputation is your reputation.

- 1 in 3 people regret something they posted online.[2]

QUICK TIP

Google your name; search results often indicate how the world sees you. Make sure to also click on the "images" and "videos" tabs to see any particular media that has been posted of you.

If you find unflattering content, you can submit a request to Google for its removal here:

www.google.com/webmasters/tools/removals

Live as Though Your Mother is Watching

- Assume whatever you do, both offline and online, will be seen by your mother, dad, boss, coach, boyfriend, teacher... the world.

- Rule of thumb: If it's something that would embarrass your mother, do not do it offline and do not post it online. Seventy percent of job recruiters in the United States report that they have rejected candidates because of information online.[3]

- Always think twice before you press the send button.

- Advances in wearable technology combined with decreasing costs of video storage indicate that soon, everything will be recorded.

- Even if you do not post your party pictures from spring break or the holiday office party, someone else will.

LEARNING MOMENTS

The world is increasingly transparent, evidenced by the fact that McDonald's secret sauce is no longer a secret. McDonald's of Canada produced a video of McDonald's executive chef Dan Coudreaut showing how to make the sauce at home.[4]

See "Secret Sauce" video: http://bit.ly/UBPMUc

· · · · ·

There were dangerous riots and looting of stores in Vancouver, Canada, following the Vancouver Canucks loss in Game 7 of the Stanley Cup hockey finals. Many looters initially escaped police punishment, but were arrested several days later.

How were they caught? Civilians helped police find wrong doers via photos that were posted on Facebook and Twitter. From these photos, "Digital Deputies" and "Digital Vigilantes" identified individuals who had committed criminal activity.

LESSON: The good outnumber the bad, always have and always will.

· · · · ·

"The people who are worried about privacy have a legitimate worry. But, we live in a complex world where you're going to have to need a level of security greater than you did back in the olden days, if you will. And, our laws and our interpretation of the Constitution, I think, have to change."

MICHAEL BLOOMBERG

· · · · ·

KISS: Keep It Super Simple

- Steve Jobs was proud of the things he and Apple decided *NOT* to do. If you try to stand for everything, then you stand for nothing. Facebook founder Mark Zuckerberg discovered that "...the trick isn't adding stuff, it's taking away."[5]

- Determine what you want to stand for as an individual, a business, a team or a family. Whether you are a sports team or a small business, you need to know your identity before you can achieve success.

- Many of us complicate our lives by trying to be everything to everyone. This makes our reputation difficult to manage. Life in the digital age is complex; those who simplify it win.

LEARNING MOMENT

A British Institute of Psychiatry study revealed that reading digital messages while performing another creative task decreases your IQ in the moment by 10 points. This decrease is the same as not sleeping for 36 hours—more than twice the impact of smoking marijuana.[6]

LESSON: Eliminating multitasking puts you on a path to simplification & success.

· · · · ·

"If you have more than three priorities, then you don't have any."

JIM COLLINS, AUTHOR OF GOOD TO GREAT

· · · · ·

· · · · ·

*"A brand for a company is like
a reputation for a person.
You earn a good reputation by trying
to do hard things well."*

JEFF BEZOS

· · · · ·

· · · · ·

*"The way to gain a good reputation
is to endeavor to be what
you desire to appear."*

SOCRATES

· · · · ·

No. 4

100% LinkedIn Profile

- LinkedIn is rapidly replacing the paper resume.

- 91% of companies use LinkedIn to research candidates.[7]

- 35% of the time recruiters find items online that cause them to dismiss a candidate.[8]

- Research from LinkedIn indicates that if your LinkedIn profile is 100% complete, you will receive **40x more job and business opportunities** than someone who doesn't have a complete profile.

- LinkedIn profiles show up high in Google search results. This is particularly helpful for those who do not have a substantial digital presence (i.e., a blog, company website, YouTube channel).

LinkedIn indicates in the upper right hand corner of your profile whether your profile is 100% complete. If it's incomplete, LinkedIn will indicate if you forgot to post a profile photo, recommendations or previous jobs.

• • • • •

"It takes 20 years to build a reputation and five minutes to ruin it. If you think about that, you'll do things differently."

WARREN BUFFETT

• • • • •

LEARNING MOMENTS

David T. Stevens signed up for LinkedIn, hoping it would help him network for his sales job with KEZR and KBAY radio in San Jose, California. Several months later, the economy took a turn for the worse, and Stevens found himself looking for work. As he headed out on his last day, he decided to post on LinkedIn, "Up for Grabs. Who wants me?"

On his ride home, he received a call from one of his contacts on LinkedIn who knew of an open job. Another LinkedIn connection recommended him to the hiring manager for this position. Stevens scheduled an interview and two weeks later, he was working for his new organization. "I was like, this is awesome," recalls Stevens, 31. "That was a miracle, but I had my doubts it could happen."[9]

· · · · ·

Surya Deepanjali experienced a traveler's nightmare. Someone grabbed Deepanjali's laptop by mistake at the Mumbai airport and he didn't' realize it until it was too late.

The only clue Deepanjali had was the company name on the other traveler's laptop. Using LinkedIn, Surya found an old classmate who worked at the same company. A few phone calls and emails later, the company was able to put Surya in contact with the traveler who mistakenly had taken his laptop to Sweden.

Hence Surya, with the help of LinkedIn, was able to locate his missing laptop 15,000 miles away and have it safely returned in two days.[10]

LESSON: It's important to be socially active, engaged and connected with powerful tools like LinkedIn. These tools can be used in a myriad of ways to benefit you both personally and professionally.

No. 5

Don't Post Whispers

- If you'd whisper it offline, do not post it online.

- If pondering whether something is appropriate to post online, ask yourself: *Would I tell this to a large group of people in-person?* If the answer is "no" or "maybe not," do not post it.

- Most whispered conversations do not reflect your best self.

- Your friends and followers will discover if you are posting whispers. You will quickly develop a reputation as someone who posts private information.

- If someone were to hear your offline whispers, they could always post it digitally.

LEARNING MOMENTS

NFL star running back Arian Foster revealed an MRI of his hamstring injury on Twitter. This is a big "no-no," since your competitors are also on Twitter and will use this injury information to their advantage in the football game.

If you work at a business and aren't sure if something is secret or proprietary, do not post it until you are 100% sure it's OK.

Do not give your competitors digital ammunition that can be later used against you.

If you hear a secret about someone or some juicy gossip, make sure it stops with you. The worst thing you can do for others and your own reputation is to post this information digitally. This will ultimately reflect poorly on you.

LESSON: Nefarious activity or secrets should be revealed; all other secrets are generally best kept secrets.

= (No. **6**) =

Integrity & Reputation are Now One

- Integrity is what you do behind closed doors or when you think nobody is watching. Integrity is the true essence of who you are, your beliefs and your values.

- Reputation is the public perception of who you are. It is how others view your integrity or strong moral principles.

- As a result of digital tools and connectivity, the difference between your integrity and reputation is now zero. Everything we do or say is broadcast to the world. The result? **Reputation = Integrity**.

LEARNING MOMENT

Meghan Vogel, a junior at Ohio's West Liberty-Salem High School, won the state's 1,600-meter race, but she became an even greater champion by finishing last in another race. Why does her last place finish have millions of views on YouTube?

In the 3,200-meter race, Vogel was 50 meters from the finish line when another runner, Arden McMath of Arlington High School, collapsed. Rather than run past her, Vogel stopped on the track and carried her fallen competitor across the finish line, making certain that McMath finished ahead of her in the race.

"Helping her across the finish line was a lot more satisfying than winning the state championship," Vogel said.

"I've never seen that," said Arlington coach Paul Hunter. "What a selfless act. That's real sportsmanship."

www.youtube.com/watch?feature=player_embedded&v=irs9XP2bplE

LESSON: Finishing first has many different definitions. Run your race.

What's Your Digital Compass?

- Write a digital compass. What do you want people to find when they search Google? Set your sights high. For example, mine is:

  Be a "Digital Dale Carnegie" by inspiring others to achieve their best life, leadership and legacy while honoring God and Family.

- Think of this as a moral compass, the guiding light for your ultimate legacy. Whenever you are faced with a difficult decision or situation, use this as your guide.

- Keep it simple—140 characters or less.

- It's helpful to write down what you want the most important people in your life to say about you at your funeral. From this exercise, you will notice you aren't writing down accomplishments (fastest, smartest, best), but more profound concepts—how did your presence uplift others? We no longer have to wait for our funeral to hear what people are saying about us. We know what people are posting about us.

Post your personal digital compass online with the hashtag #digitalcompass

ACTION ITEM

LEARNING MOMENT

At the young age of three, Dyrk Burcie was diagnosed with pediatric liver cancer. Dyrk's father was a firefighter and Dyrk certainly had the fighting spirit. This spirit soon became known as "Dyrk Strong." As Dyrk battled this terminal disease, local fire stations started posting images of "Dyrk" and "Dyrk Strong."

The fire stations looked for unique ways to send their support for this courageous boy. Fire stations became creative by spelling the name "Dyrk" letter-by-letter in fire or casting it alongside the tallest ladder on the fire truck.

Soon, the cause spread globally, with thousands of people posting images dedicated to Dyrk and his cancer prevention cause. Dyrk's courage showcases that in today's digital era, mountains can be moved and hearts can be connected as the communication barriers of time and distance are removed.

Dyrk died in peace after his fourth birthday, but his digital legacy lives on forever.

More on Dyrk: http://bit.ly/dyrk-strong

LESSON: Take inspiration from our hero Dyrk by leaving a legacy that matters.

· · · · ·

"We don't get a chance to do that many things, and everyone should be really excellent. Because this is our life ... life is brief, and then you die, you know?"

STEVE JOBS

· · · · ·

Be FLAWsome

- The world is a better place because of everyone's imperfections.

- Admit and own your flaws either as an organization or as an individual and the world will think you are awesome.

- Being "Flawsome" [11] is admitting that you aren't perfect. You are awesome because of your flaws. Flawsome is described as owning your mistakes and taking the necessary steps to correct them. It's about turning a negative into a positive (such as making digital lemonade out of digital lemons).

- Making a mistake as a business or as an individual is your opportunity to show customers and followers that you are awesome by caring enough to correct the flaw. 83% of customers liked or loved that a brand responded to a complaint on Twitter. Yet, 76% of people who complain on Twitter do not receive a response from the brand. [12]

LEARNING MOMENTS

A young woman at the Red Cross thought she was posting to her own Twitter account, but accidentally hit the button for the Red Cross Twitter account. She posted *"Ryan found two more 4 packs of Dogfish Head's Midas Touch beer, when we drink we do it right."* A young man at the Red Cross saw this mistake and immediately posted on Twitter *"We've deleted the rogue tweet, but rest assured the Red Cross is sober and we've confiscated the keys."* [13]

The result? The beer company suggested that instead of drinking a pint of beer, beer drinkers should consider donating a pint of blood to the Red Cross. Donations for the Red Cross increased dramatically that week. By using humor, the Red Cross showed they are simply people trying to help people. They turned a potential negative situation into a positive one. They were Flawsome!

I too witnessed this first hand. Some of my most ardent literary critics often become my biggest supporters when I listen to what they say and admit that I made a grammatical error or acknowledge that a chapter in the book isn't "up to snuff."

FedEx also discovered that a customer is three times more likely to remain a steady customer when resolving a customer's complaint, as compared to a person who never experienced a problem with FedEx.

LESSON: Rather than attempting to present a perfect digital profile, proudly present yourself—*"here I am, warts and all!"* Also, speed wins. A quick, short response in four minutes is better than the perfect response four days later.

More on Flawsome here:
http://www.trendwatching.com/trends/flawsome/

*Hat tip: Ann Handley first introduced me to this concept

═ (№. 9) ═

Privacy is Your Problem

- Do not assume that someone else is looking out for your digital privacy.

- Facebook, Twitter and even the FBI (see below), despite their best intentions and privacy tools, do not care nearly as much about your privacy as you should.

- Therefore, you need to take ownership of your privacy and identity. Stay abreast of security breaches involving companies you use.

- Pay attention to emails discussing security breaches, but never click on these emails, as they could be phishing scams. Instead, visit the company site directly by typing in the Web address. This will save you from accidentally clicking on a phishing scam, including fake emails or websites attempting to obtain your personal information.

- Periodically review free credit rating reports from the appropriate agencies in your country. These credit reports often can alert you to a potential digital security breach involving your personal data.

ACTION ITEM

Review the passwords you have set for your accounts. If there are any passwords that someone could easily guess (i.e., password, 12345, your last name), take a moment to change them.

LEARNING MOMENT

The Antisec hacker group reported stealing 12 million Apple IDs from the computer of an FBI agent. This hacker group then posted the personal information of some of these IDs online.[14]

LESSON: If the FBI can be hacked, so can you.

· · · · ·

"Once you've lost your privacy, you realize you've lost an extremely valuable thing."

BILLY GRAHAM

· · · · ·

Have One Digital Identity

- Multiple online accounts for the same service result in multiple personalities. This complexity can eventually cause your downfall.

- With rare exceptions, it is best to have only one account/ profile for each digital network, including avoiding having four different Facebook profiles. Having only one account is also easier to maintain—and less stressful (see rule #3 Simplify)!

- Many people have discovered that having a LinkedIn account for their business contacts and a Facebook account for their personal contacts is a great approach. If you aren't comfortable when your boss wants to connect with you on Facebook, kindly ask him/her to connect with you on LinkedIn and encourage your boss to write you a LinkedIn recommendation! Keep in mind, like it or not, the days of having a work personality and a completely different weekend personality are over.

- Be yourself! It is much easier than pretending to be someone else. The rules in this book are guidelines; they aren't designed to make you a robot. Let your own unique personality shine online.

· · · · ·

"Privacy is one of the biggest problems in this new electronic age."

ANDY GROVE

· · · · ·

· · · · ·

"I have as much privacy as a goldfish in a bowl."

PRINCESS MARGARET

· · · · · ·

LEARNING MOMENTS

The FBI uncovered U.S. Central Intelligence Director General David Petraeus's trail of deceit and extramarital affair. Petraeus and U.S. Army Lieutenant, Paula Broadwell, were having an affair. Despite Petraeus's expansive knowledge of digital espionage, the FBI was eventually able to find some digital breadcrumbs indicting the two. Petraeus and Broadwell had set up a communication system using fake names via free webmail accounts and exchanged messages without encryption tools. They would share an email account with one saving a message in the draft's folder and the other deleting the message after it was read.[15]

This was one of the biggest scandals in history and Petraeus was forced to tender his resignation as Director of the CIA to President Barack Obama.

LESSON: If the Director of the CIA can't cover his tracks, do not think you will succeed in leading a double life.

· · · · ·

"You have one identity. The days of you having a different image for your work friends or co-workers and for the other people you know are probably coming to an end pretty quickly… Having two identities for yourself is an example of a lack of integrity."[16]

— Mark Zuckerberg, Facebook Founder & CEO

LESSON: The days of different personalities for different friends and groups are over.

Complain = Digital Pain

- Complaining is negative energy and the enemy of greatness.

- Remember: Anything you post online is in "ink," not "pencil." Do you want your digital footprint littered with complaints?

- It's imperative not to complain about a particular person. Think how you feel when you see a post that says, "<your name> is a jerk!"

- The average person complains 15-30 times per day. You can positively stand out simply by not complaining.

· · · · ·

*"If you don't like something,
change it.
If you can't change it,
change your attitude.
Don't complain."*

MAYA ANGELOU

· · · · ·

LEARNING MOMENT

A young man was working for an online agency and Chrysler was their marquee client. Part of his job was to assist Chrysler with its Twitter account. On one particular day, he had a very difficult commute to work.

To help relieve his frustration, he posted to his Twitter account, *"I find it ironic that Detroit is known as the #motorcity and yet no one here knows how to fu***** drive."* Unfortunately, he hit the wrong button and instead of posting to his private Twitter account, he posted this on the Chrysler Twitter account for millions to see. He and his agency where quickly fired.[17] Complaining often negatively impacts the complainer, so rise above it.

The average person complains 15-30 times per day.[18] Be above average—stop complaining.

A good way to practice not complaining is to track your progress. For each complaint-free day, put a rubber band on your wrist. Try to accumulate seven days in a row without a complaint. Good luck!

LESSON: Be wary of texting and tweeting in the heat of the moment.

Post It Forward

- You have heard the expression pay it forward: performing good deeds without expecting something in return. Digital tools like Twitter, Facebook and LinkedIn make it easy to praise someone digitally.

- Make a daily habit of posting daily a positive comment about someone via a blog, Twitter, text, Facebook or email. There are only upsides.

- Research shows that posting positive items about others increases your own happiness.[19]

- Religiously use the *Endorse, Like, Re-pin, 1+* and *Follow* buttons to make someone's day.

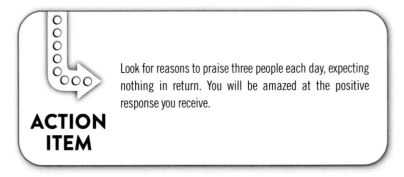

Look for reasons to praise three people each day, expecting nothing in return. You will be amazed at the positive response you receive.

ACTION ITEM

LEARNING MOMENT

I loved a particular song by Christopher Tin and wanted to use it for a YouTube video I was creating. Tin embraced the idea that I was creating awareness of his music with my loyal followers. We exchanged signed copies of books for signed copies of music and posted pleasant things about one another digitally. Tin's incredible talents eventually enabled him to win two Grammy's. While we expected nothing in return by "posting it forward," each of us experienced long-term benefits.

LESSON: A one-second positive post will brighten someone's day and could brighten yours for many years to come.

· · · · ·

"A life lived for others, is the only life worth living."

ALBERT EINSTEIN

· · · · ·

= (No. 13) =

Network Before You Need Your Network

- Individuals do not achieve success in a vacuum. In order to reach your goals, you need to stand on the shoulders of others.

- Those who succeed develop deep relationships before they need those relationships. They network before they need the network both offline and online. A candidate tracking study showed networking was the most effective method for obtaining a new job.[20]

- It's difficult to ask for a favor when you haven't communicated with or previously helped that other person.

- Online networks like LinkedIn make it easy to build new relationships or strengthen existing relationships.

- When you do make a digital mistake, your network will help support you and mitigate the damage.

- Social media has diminished the gatekeeper to industry leaders. It's now easier than ever to reach out to your role model and receive a response.

· · · · ·

"Surround yourself with people who are smarter than you."

RUSSELL SIMMONS

· · · · ·

LEARNING MOMENT

The city of Grand Rapids, Michigan was experiencing some challenging times when Newsweek wrote an article declaring it a "Dying City." In response, the entire Grand Rapids community rallied to produce the world's largest lip dub video, singing along to Don McLean's famous song "American Pie." Sponsors covered the $40,000 production cost and over 5,000 people volunteered.

The video has received millions of views and at one point was one of the Top 10 most viewed videos on YouTube. Roger Ebert called it "the greatest music video ever made."

View video here: http://bit.ly/am-pie

LESSON: ONE is never stronger than MANY, offline or online.

$$= \left(\begin{array}{c} \mathcal{N}o. \\ \mathbf{14} \end{array} \right) =$$

Praise Publicly, Criticize Privately

- Never criticize your boss, mom, teacher, rabbi or coach; the worst thing you can do is to criticize publicly, especially through digital outlets.

- If you have an issue with someone, address it as quickly as possible in person. If face-to-face isn't an option, then set up a time for discussion by phone or via video conversation. Make sure your settings are set for private, not public. It is always preferable to handle conflict face-to-face.

- Sometimes our emotions get in the way of our common sense. Even the most sensible people can be caught up in the emotions of an argument with a co-worker or a negative reaction to a comment their friend made. It's often in the heat of the moment that people post things they often regret after having some time to cool down.

- If you have something positive to say about someone or something, post away! Post it forward (Rule #11).

LEARNING MOMENT

Kevin Curwick, a Minnesota High School student and football team captain, uses Twitter for good. Curwick set up the anonymous account @OsseoNiceThings to help counterattack cyberbullies. Whenever a student is attacked by cyberbullies, Curwick posts nice things about the victim to help boost that student's confidence.

The movement has been able to uplift people across the United States, Australia and England. Curwick revealed that he was the person behind the account on KARE-TV in Minneapolis-St. Paul.[21] Since this public announcement, he has since received high praise from teachers, students, potential colleges and even Ryan Seacrest. It has resulted in a "nice page" movement in other towns and cities.

LESSON: Be the link in the chain that breaks the pattern of malicious acts like cyberbullying.

• • • • •

"The nicest feeling in the world is to do a good deed anonymously-and have somebody find out."

OSCAR WILDE

• • • • •

• • • • •

"In the future, we will all enjoy our 15 minutes of privacy."

SCOTT MONTY, FORD

• • • • •

No. 15

Measure Twice, Post Once

- A good carpenter measures twice and hammers once. We too must read our words twice and post just once. While it may take extra time in the short term, it will save time in the long-term.

- This also can be applied to blogging. Be sure to read your posts thoroughly for grammatical and spelling errors. Even the most thoughtful posts can be ruined if they are littered with errors or incorrect data.

- Short and powerful comments are usually best.

LEARNING MOMENT

Cardale Jones, a quarterback on the Ohio State University football team, made his feelings about attending classes clear on Twitter.

"Why should we have to go to class if we came here to play FOOTBALL, we ain't come to play SCHOOL classes are POINTLESS," he posted.

Embarrassed, OSU officials publicly reminded all of their athletes, "Always remember not to post or tweet anything that could embarrass themselves, their team, teammates, the university, their family or other groups, organizations or people."[22]

LESSON: A valuable team member does not act selfishly. Inappropriate expressions of opinion reflect poorly on the team, whether they are shared on the field, off the field or through online outlets.

No. 16

The Three-Second Rule

- If you have to think for more than three seconds about whether something is appropriate—it's not.

- Read the above bullet point—then read it again!

LEARNING MOMENT

Nokia produced a polished television commercial for the launch of a new mobile phone. The commercial showcased the new stabilization feature of the phone's video camera.

A young, attractive couple is bike riding in Europe and the young man films the young woman as they ride. Like diet advertisements that utilize before and after photos, the commercial showcased video footage with the stabilization feature off, highlighting a bumpy ride and with the stabilization feature on, highlighting a smooth ride with clear imagery.

The smooth footage in the commercial wasn't the result of the Nokia camera. Rather, the commercial was filmed using a sophisticated high-definition movie camera mounted on a tripod in a van traveling alongside the bikes! How was Nokia caught in this deceptive act?

During the sequence, for a split second, the couple biked in front of a glass window. In that brief moment, someone slowed the video and the camera van was visible in the reflection! Nokia immediately issued a public apology and withdrew the million-dollar commercial.[23]

LESSON: Companies and teams must foster a culture of openness and encourage all staff—from junior analyst to executives—to raise a red flag when items appear untruthful or morally corrupt. Everybody benefits in an open, transparent environment.

No. 17

We Will Make Digital Mistakes; How We Handle Them is What Defines Us

- It's not a question of *if* we will make an online or offline mistake, the question is when and how we handle it.

- How we handle these mistakes (with integrity) is what ultimately separates and defines our digital stamp.

- Often it's not the crime, but the cover-up that gets us into trouble. (see rule #20)

LEARNING MOMENTS

Married Congressman Anthony Weiner was accused of sending lewd tweets and photos to several women, including college students, while he and his wife were expecting their first child.

Weiner vehemently denied any wrongdoing and stated, "I know for a fact that my account was hacked. I can definitively say that I did not send this."[24]

Unfortunately for Weiner, a few women released to the press inappropriate photos they had received from him. One photo showcased Weiner surrounded by family photos, holding a piece of paper with the word "me" and an arrow pointing towards him. Another photo of Weiner wearing underwear was particularly damaging. Late night talk show hosts had a field day using the Congressman's last name as grist for their comedy routine.

Weiner finally admitted he hadn't been hacked. He acknowledged that he sent photos and engaged in inappropriate communication with multiple women over a three-year period. Weiner was forced to resign from Congress.

Sadly, once he was caught, he continued his inappropriate digital communication with several women. This cost him an election bid in a later campaign.

LESSON: Illicit digital acts can result in job loss and disgrace.

= (No. **18**) =

Multitasking = Mistakes

- Automobile accidents often occur because one or both drivers were distracted. *Car & Driver Magazine's* research found that compared to a baseline of attentive driving, impaired drivers traveling at 70 MPH (103 feet/second) took 8 feet longer to react to danger and begin braking their vehicle. By contrast, test results showed that texting drivers took 40 feet longer to react and begin braking. Thus, the texting drivers reacted 5 times slower than the impaired drivers did.

- Digital mistakes often occur because the sender was distracted. Focus on one item at a time and the potential for a digital "oops" moment is lessened. Multitaskers make up to 50% more errors.[25]

- Multiple studies demonstrate that people are healthier and more productive when they DO NOT multi-task. Neuroscience reveals that our brain doesn't have the ability to multi-task like a computer. Rather, we switch between tasks requiring our brain to decide which task is more important. Time and energy costs are associated with each of these switches.

- Gary Small, a neuroscientist and author of the book iBrain, warns that children who spend their formative years multitasking lose out on chances to focus on developing crucial but slow-forming interpersonal skills.[26]

LEARNING MOMENT

Experts Joshua Rubinstein, PhD, Jeffrey Evans, PhD and David Meyer, PhD, estimate that switching between tasks can decrease productivity by 40 percent. Errors can result, especially if one is working on items that involve a lot of critical thinking. [27]

One in five pedestrian teenagers admitted to being distracted by their mobile device when they were treated in the emergency room after being hit by an automobile.[28]

A study by the British Institute of Psychology concluded that our IQ drops by 10 points each time we multi-task, equivalent to staying awake for 36 hours, which is twice the effect of smoking marijuana.[29]

LESSON: Multi-tasking makes us less efficient, more prone to make mistakes, stresses our health and can even result in serious injury.

No. 19

Honesty is Easy

- Honesty is easy and liberating. You always remember the truth!

- Trustworthiness is the sister of honesty. The quickest way to lose the faith of your boss, teammate, teacher, parent or coach is to disclose information publicly entrusted to you. Do what is right even when it's difficult. Keep Promises. Be true to yourself. Show up on time and honor your commitments. Under-promise and over-deliver.

· · · · ·

"Honesty is the first chapter in the book of wisdom."

THOMAS JEFFERSON

· · · · ·

LEARNING MOMENTS

Four students approached their professor and apologized for missing a very important exam. They explained that a flat tire was the cause of their tardiness. In response to their request for a make-up exam, the professor said, "No problem. You can all take the exam together tomorrow." The students arrived the next day and the professor explained, "This is a pass/fail exam. Either all four of you will pass or all four of you will fail." She handed one blank sheet of paper to each student and placed them in separate corners. "We only have one question today," she stated, "Which tire?"

• • • • •

A U.S. employee of Anglo-Irish Bank asked his boss for a personal day to address a family matter. Someone then posted the employee's photo on Facebook. He was in attendance at a party holding a wand and wearing a tutu. All his colleagues discovered the lie.

LESSON: Don't lie to your boss; don't lie to anyone. Don't wear a tutu.

• • • • •

Google sets trap for Microsoft: Google had a suspicion that Microsoft's search engine Bing was stealing and mirroring the search results from Google. Google made up several fake words and seeded them into the Google search results. Sure enough, these fictitious results soon appeared on Bing's search engine.[30]

LESSON: Companies sometimes achieve short-term gains through deceit or deception. When these dishonorable practices are discovered, the companies always pay a steep price.

It's Not the Crime, But the Cover-Up

We all make mistakes and must face those online and offline mistakes head on. The next time you make a mistake:

- Own it
- Apologize
- Lay out action items and public steps to "make it right"
- Follow through on these steps
- Learn from the experience

LEARNING MOMENT

Jim Tressel, the National Champion football coach of Ohio State University, found himself in a difficult situation. His sterling reputation was under attack. Several of the team's most prominent players were accused of selling school issued memorabilia in exchange for body tattoos. Body art or tattoos are considered a form of monetary value, a direct violation of NCAA rules.

Tressel thanked the NCAA for uncovering these incidents and stated he was unaware of any such activity. Emails were later uncovered indicating Tressel had been informed of this illegal activity and did nothing to stop it. Once the emails were released, Tressel was fired for lying to the NCAA officials. In retrospect, the infractions by the players were considered minor violations and Ohio State and Tressel would have received a very light penalty had they initially acknowledged wrongdoing and asked for forgiveness. Tressel's attempt to cover-up the crime ultimately resulted in his fall from grace.

LESSON: Honesty is always the best policy, especially when you make a major mistake.

Make Ginormous Public Goals

- Set goals and share them with others. When others know your goals, they are in position to support you in achieving them.

- Goals are important. Jason DeAmato, author of *For Sales*, states, "Imagine basketball without any goals. You'd simply be running around the court and passing the ball."

- I'm sure some of us have experienced this lack of focus after a long day. Make sure to hang goals at each end of your court.

LEARNING MOMENT

A child battled infant acute lymphoblastic leukemia soon after her birth. Doctors searched tirelessly to locate a bone marrow donor to match her rare blood type. After making an appeal through social media, more than 5,400 people signed up globally as potential donors. A match was eventually found in Australia.[31]

LESSON: Most people want to help others. Let them help you by publicly posting your goals. If others do not know your goals, they can't help you achieve them.

· · · · ·

"Three things cannot be long hidden: the sun, the moon, and the truth."

BUDDHA

· · · · ·

Face-2-Face Cannot Be Replaced

- 93% of communication is non-verbal. If you are spending all your time communicating via a screen, you are doing yourself a tremendous disservice.[32]

- Research indicates people are twice as likely to remember you if you shake hands. The research also shows that people with whom you shake hands will respond in a friendlier and more open manner.[33]

- 88% of people believe others are less polite on social media than in person.[34]

- Our tone in digital messages is misinterpreted 50 percent of the time.[35]

- Developing your network requires online *and* offline interaction. Digital tools are incredible when time and distance are an issue, but you can never replace face-2-face interactions.

LEARNING MOMENT

A Mom asking one of her two daughters for help via texting:[36]

Messages **Mom** Edit

Call FaceTime Contact >

"What does IDK, LY & TTYL mean?"

I don't know, love you, talk to you later.

OK, I will ask your sister.

LESSON: Since digital conversations lack verbal cues, it's always best to make sure you are specific and straightforward.

$\equiv$ (*No.* **23**) $\equiv$

Tinderbox Topics—Caution!

- These subjects often cause incendiary reaction, especially within digital text where we do not have the context of nonverbal cues. When approaching these topics, use extreme caution: Politics and Religion

- When discussing tinderbox topics, it's generally best to support your position via fact-based perspectives, rather than emotionally charged ones. The top five controversial topics on Wikipedia are: George Bush, Anarchism, Muhammed, Pro Wrestling and Global Warming.[37]

- The best way to diffuse an argument is to agree. While you may not agree with 90% of an opposition's position, you may agree with 10%. You gain credibility with the undecided group when you acknowledge minimal agreement. This shows strength, which supports your efforts to convince the undecided group that your viewpoint has merit.

- Sometimes the best response is silence.

- Pride in your religion is glorious; trying to convert everyone via digital posts is not glorious.

LEARNING MOMENT

SECRET SERVICE BORED: A member of the secret service mistakenly thought he was posting to his own Twitter account, but instead his disapproval of Fox News went out on behalf of the entire secret service: "Had to monitor Fox for a story. Can't. Deal. With. The. Blathering."

LESSON: Know your professional position and understand that while your friends may post something on a particular topic, you may not have this same luxury based on your job, position, team or company.

The Power of a Letter

- How do you feel when you receive another email? How do you feel when you receive a handwritten letter in the mail? A nice handwritten letter makes your day. Make someone's day.

- In our world of tweeting, texting and emailing, a letter will get you noticed. Be unique. Stand out. Personal handwritten notes grow rarer by the day. According to the U.S. Postal Service's annual survey, the average home only received a personal letter once every seven weeks in 2010, down from once every two weeks in 1987. Whereas the average business e-mail account sends and receives over 100 e-mails daily and the younger generation sends over 100 texts daily.[38]

- Next time you make a mistake, take the time to send a letter. It is significantly more personal than email and shows that you truly care.

ACTION ITEM

Who is someone you have not spoken with in a while? Is there a colleague that helped you with a project at work? A coach who was instrumental in your long-term success? Identify someone in your life and reach out to him or her with a letter or card.

LEARNING MOMENT

A CEO of a Fortune 500 company invited me to deliver a keynote to a room full of Fortune 1000 CEOs. I was so grateful that I sent a handwritten thank you note. My wife and I also sent his family a Christmas card.

Several months later, I received a call from the Dean at the McCombs School of Business asking me to deliver the commencement address to that year's graduating MBA class. I was surprised and delighted. It was an honor to return to the Austin campus where I had received my MBA. This incredible opportunity seemed to come from nowhere. I learned later that I was strongly recommended by that Fortune 500 CEO.

LESSON: You will never regret taking the time to write someone a personal letter... on paper.

Cyberbullying: Don't Enable It

- Cyberbullying is defined as teasing, insulting or making fun of another person online. The intent is often to soil the target's reputation. If you are a cyberbully, STOP! Your bullying could be the byproduct of social anxiety or low self-esteem and it is important that you seek help. Teachers, friends, parents and school counselors are increasingly aware of the signs of cyberbullying and will eventually confront you. Cyberbullying is often considered a criminal offense and offline bullying laws apply to online behavior.

- Teens are not the only victims of cyberbullying. Adults are attacked as well.

- Cyberbullies leave digital fingerprints and often are easier to prosecute than traditional bullies who do not leave as much incriminating evidence.

- Bullying can ultimately lead to a victim's suicide. Victims of cyberbullying are twice as likely to commit suicide as those who have not had a cyberbullying experience.

- 1 in 7 students is either a bully or a victim of bullying.[39]

LEARNING MOMENTS

Tyler Clementi, a male 18-year-old New Jersey student, was caught on a hidden camera kissing another man. The roommate who filmed the couple threatened to circulate the video. He then followed through on his threat by posting it several times on Twitter and then on YouTube. Clementi, overwhelmed, committed suicide by jumping into a river. Clementi was a victim of cyberbullying.[40]

• • • • •

Rebecca Marino, a professional tennis player, after receiving threats on social media sites, announced her resignation from the sport. "Go die" and "burn in hell" were among the threatening messages.[41] Rebecca Marino has since deleted her social media accounts.

LESSON: If you witness cyberbullying or traditional bullying and choose to do nothing, you are an enabler and an accomplice to the bully. Your silence encourages the bully to continue. Choose to be a leader and give a voice to those who do not have one. Take the high road and help someone in need. If the situation were reversed, you would want someone to stand up for you! Do not be a bystander, be an "upstander."

NOTE: The process of 'coming out' for an individual that identifies as LGBTQ, can be very difficult. Just because someone comes out to you in person, doesn't mean he or she is ready for it to be broadcast to the Internet. See rule #5; don't post whispers.

$$= \left(\substack{\mathcal{N}o. \\ \mathbf{26}} \right) =$$

See Your Kids as Others See Them

- The way your children behave at home might be entirely different from the way they behave around others.

- Show your children what is right and wrong by providing them examples (see *Learning Moment* video below) and taking the time to explain the concepts in this book.

- Our kids are growing up in a different time than we did. I am sure we have all done things in our childhood or as a teenager that we are glad is not online. Now, our kids are learning about who they want to be and who they can trust, all while living in a fishbowl. It's important to show your kids the perception they are giving to others by their online identities, and how that perception compares to who they hope to be.

- Stay active in your children's digital lives and stress that digital access including Internet access and payment for their phone is a privilege, not a right. As part of this privilege, they need to be connected to you on various networks (e.g. friends on Facebook) and be aware that you will monitor their smart phone usage (e.g. texts).

LEARNING MOMENT

Four 13-year-old boys bullied Karen Klein, a 68-year-old grandmother and school bus monitor, in Rochester, NY. A video, recorded via an iPhone, revealed the students calling Klein a "f$#% fat, ugly and a sweaty troll." They jabbed her incessantly with their fingers as she wept uncontrollably.

One student taunted, "You don't have a family because they all killed themselves because they don't want to be near you." Klein's oldest son killed himself 10 years prior.

This ugly bus incident went viral on YouTube, receiving more than 1.8 million views within two days. Klein was surprised to learn the video was posted online and even more surprised by the support she received from strangers throughout the world. "Strangers stopped and they give me hugs," Klein said. "I've been overwhelmed by supportive emails, Facebook messages and flowers."

A Toronto man, Max Sidorov, who was a victim of bullying as a young immigrant from Ukraine, noted that Klein only earns $15,506 a year. He set a goal to raise $5,000 for her to take a much-needed holiday. Within a few days, he had raised $375,000. Sidorov hopes Klein can use the money to retire.[42]

A father of one of the tormentors offered her a sincere apology and indicated a written apology from his son would be forthcoming. All four boys were placed under police security, since they received numerous death threats. One of the 13-year-old boys received over 1,000 missed calls and 1,000 threatening text messages.[43]

Klein didn't press initial charges and hopes the kids learned a lesson and will act respectfully in the future.

Video of incident:
www.youtube.com/watch?v=E12R9fMMtos

Summary on NBC Today Show:
www.youtube.com/watch?v=668AQoumzWo&feature=related

LESSON: The same tools that are used for cyberbullying can be used to disable traditional bullying and reward and uplift a victim.

No. 27

Be authentic

- There is only one you. Be yourself. Be authentic.

- Customers reward businesses that are open and authentic. According to the ALOFT Group, a study by Napoli, et al., found that brand authenticity is a better predictor of purchase intentions than brand love, trust or credibility. [44]

LEARNING MOMENTS

Married Republican Christopher Lee sent a topless picture of himself to a woman he met on a 'Women Seeking Men' forum on craigslist.org. "I'm a very fit, fun and classy guy. Live in Cap Hill area. 6ft 190lbs blond/blue. 39. Lobbyist. I promise not to disappoint."

Those disappointed were his wife and young son. Lee even lied about his age (he was 46 not 39). Lee resigned from his congressional post.

LESSON: We do not live in an era of Mad Men where lying and cheating activities are easily undetected.

* * * * *

On Gay Pride Day, Oreo posted an image of their iconic chocolate wafer cookie on social media. This made news because the traditional white cream filling was replaced with the color of the rainbow and the word "Pride" beneath it. This support of the gay community was controversial, but it was authentic in what Oreo believes in. The campaign won numerous awards and the positives outweighed the negatives. Specifically, Oreo doubled their daily fans from 25,000 per day to 50,000 per day, helping them approach 40 million likes on Facebook. They also had 80,000 people share the post, which equated to a 4929% increase over normal sharing activity for Oreo.[45]

Fail Fast, Fail Forward, Fail Better

- As entrepreneurs, individuals or organizations, the rapid pace of digital expansion means that our initiatives might fail the first time. In fact, failure may result more frequently than success.

- The fastest way to increase our rate of learning in the digital era is to increase our rate of failure.

- Failing better is the ability to detect when a construct just isn't right for the current situation. Successful people know how to pivot an idea or business plan quickly. They pivot toward something that may prove more successful than their original plan. For example, 3Ms Post-It Notes were the result of a failed glue design.

- A recent survey by American Express showed the top three characteristics of "influencers" are:
  - Confidence
  - Education
  - The willingness to try new things

- Go ahead, try new things and do not worry about failing.

LEARNING MOMENT

Wine and liquor storeowner Gary Vaynerchuk of the Wine Library had 12 people watch his first YouTube wine show. These viewers believed the format was stuffy and traditional and encouraged him to take advantage of his outgoing New Jersey personality and develop a more entertaining format. Gary listened to his fan base. The Wine Library became one of the most viral shows on YouTube and sales increased from $4 million annually to over $50 million. Gary is now a best-selling author, media company owner and keynote speaker.

LESSON: Don't easily give up on a good idea if it doesn't work the first time. It might eventually make you $50 million dollars.

• • • • •

"You can't build a reputation on what you are going to do."

HENRY FORD

• • • • •

Freedom of Choice— Not Freedom From Consequence

- Despite our loss of privacy, we still have the freedom of choice. You may tattoo the devil on your forehead but limit your ability to secure employment, a significant consequence.

- Our online and offline choices impact our employer, family, friends, everyone. These choices often determine whether we are hired or fired, liked or disliked, promoted or demoted.

LEARNING MOMENT

When Evan Wilder was knocked from his bike by a reckless car, he was more concerned with his life than getting the license plate of the hit-and-run driver. Witnesses were unavailable. However, the video camera that Wilder had affixed to his bike helmet proved helpful. After watching the video recording, police were able to locate and apprehend the guilty driver.[46]

LESSON: We have choices. Will we lift someone up or knock someone down?

• • • • •

You take unacceptable risk, you have to be prepared to face the consequence.

CARLY FIORINA

• • • • • •

Adhere to the Golden Rule

- We tried to keep the rules in this book simple. Lest you forget them all, you will have much digital success if you adhere to the Golden Rule:

BUDDHISM: Hurt not others in ways that you yourself would find hurtful.

CHRISTIANITY: Do unto others what you would have them do unto you; this sums up the Law and the Prophets.

HINDUISM: This is the sum of duty: do naught unto others that would cause you pain if done to you.

ISLAM: No one of you is a believer until he desires for his brother that which he desires for himself.

JUDAISM: What is hateful to you, do not to your fellow man. That is the entire law; all the rest is commentary.

· · · · ·

"Associate with men of good quality
if you esteem your own reputation;
for it is better to be alone
than in bad company."

GEORGE WASHINGTON

· · · · ·

LEARNING MOMENTS

Delroy Simmonds was waiting for a New York City subway when a huge gust of wind engulfed the station. The wind violently tossed a baby onto the lower platform as an unstoppable train barreled down, blaring its horn. In shock, the baby's mother and bystanders, stood frozen. Simmonds, a father of two, jumped down onto the track and grabbed the baby seconds before the train reached the baby.

Simmons had been out of work for over a year and missed a job interview because of his heroic act. However, national and digital media spread news of his heroism and a job offer came a few days later.[47]

Simmonds shrugged off the label of hero, "I'm just a normal person. Anybody in that situation would have done what I did."

LESSON: Do good for others and others will do good for you, both online and offline.

No. 31

You Represent Your Company, Organization & Family

- The ability to have separate personalities and behaviors for your work life versus your private life no longer exists. This shift is permanent and we need to embrace new challenges and opportunities.

- Positive and negative choices not only impact your digital reputation, but also your company, co-workers, church, family...everyone with whom you associate. The world has shifted. It is now interconnected and your actions may have unintended consequences.

LEARNING MOMENTS

Comedian Gilbert Gottfried started tweeting jokes about Japan right after tens of thousands were killed by the 2011 Tsunami. It cost him his job as the voice of the Aflac duck.

LESSON: Digital sarcasm focusing on catastrophic events is always unwise. Your postings have the power to help or harm those with whom you associate.

$\equiv$ No. 32 $\equiv$

Be a Baker, not an Eater

- Because of the stress and fast-paced nature of today's world, as a survival instinct, we often will take on an internal focus. This internal focus often looks like this: *What do I need to get done? What is this activity doing for me?* However, if we all take the time *to be kinder than we need to be*, not only will we make the world a better place, but we will start to see others help us more too.

- As author Guy Kawasaki stresses, be a *Baker*, not an *Eater*. A baker understands that more pies can always be made. An *Eater* upon seeing someone else eat a slice of pie immediately thinks, *"Hey, there will be less for me...I better eat as much pie as I can now."*

LEARNING MOMENT

An airline gate attendant was curt with passengers, and in some instances, rude. It was obvious she didn't want to be working. In return for her unpleasantness, people posted negative comments online about the airline service and her unprofessional behavior.

An elderly woman in front of me kindly said to her, "Listen dear, I know something else must be bothering you." Tears rolled down the attendant's face when she sobbed, "It's my little boy. He is very sick and in the children's hospital. My husband is so distressed that he can't work at his construction job so I have to work extra hours here to help pay the medical bills, when I should be taking care of my son." From there, customers and co-workers within hearing distance were sympathetic and shifted their attitudes to help the gate attendant positively in her time of distress.

LESSON: Always try to see everyone in the best light. The healthy do not require a helping hand or to be healed. The weak and the sick need help. Anger is often an outward manifestation of pain or sadness.

· · · · ·

"Character is like a tree and reputation like a shadow. The shadow is what we think of it; the tree is the real thing."

ABRAHAM LINCOLN

· · · · ·

No. 33

Your Legacy =
Digital Footprint + Digital Shadows

- 92% of children under the age of two have a digital shadow.[48]

- Digital Footprint = items you upload about yourself.

- Digital Shadow = items that others post about you.

- Digital Stamp = the summary of information people will learn about you today and 300 years from now digitally, your digital legacy. Digital Stamp = Digital Footprints + Shadows.

LEARNING MOMENTS

Whitney Kropp, a Michigan high school student, was the victim of a cruel prank. As a joke, her classmates voted to include her to be on homecoming court. At the encouragement of her family, Kropp held her head high, faced her bullies and remained on the court.

News of the prank spread and local residents rallied behind Kropp. Businesses donated a homecoming dress, shoes and free salon styling. A Facebook page in her honor was created and received over 100,000 likes from around the globe.

"It is absolutely awesome to see her stand up," beamed her mother, Bernice Kropp, "and it's so cool to see the messages we're getting from all over how Whitney's story has helped and touched them. My daughter is out there as an inspiration to a lot of people, and it's a really cool thing."[49] Whitney posted a video on YouTube to thank her supporters and it went viral.

LESSON: Often the best way to combat a negative force is to stand up to that force and shine a light on it.

No. 34

Surround yourself with success

- A critical item to success is to surround oneself with the right people both offline and online (for online, we strongly suggest LinkedIn). 15% of the reason a person gets a job, keeps a job, or advances in a job is related to technical skills and job knowledge; 85% has to do with people skills.[50]

- Remind your supporters how important and valued they are to you by giving them digital hugs and digital bouquets—do not forget the real hugs and flowers either!

- Pay attention to cues from your support network regarding what you do well and what you do poorly.

• • • • •

"Your reputation is in the hands of others. That's what a reputation is. You can't control that. The only thing you can control is your character."

WAYNE W. DYER

• • • • •

LEARNING MOMENTS

Seven-year-old Jack Hoffman lived a dream when he was called onto the Nebraska Huskers' football field. Dressed in football pads and a little red Nebraska football jersey, Jack made a symbolic 69-yard touchdown run. The play became the Video of the Week on ESPN and it received over eight million YouTube views. President Obama even paid Jack a personal visit.

You see, Jack was diagnosed with pediatric brain cancer in April of 2011 and undergone multiple surgeries and chemotherapy.[51] Rex Burkhead, Nebraska's running back, became fast friends with Jack. Burkhead, Captain of "Team Jack," was instrumental in getting Jack on the field for his historic run. Sixty thousand fans stood and cheered as loud as they do for their National Championship Teams. It was a day Jack will never forget.

Burkhead said after the emotional run, "Jack is a fighter, a strong kid. To see him run around and enjoy the Husker experience, it's a dream come true, especially for kids in the state of Nebraska. For Jack to get down here and do it, I know it made his day." Jack said that the moment "felt awesome."[52]

The Nebraska football team understood Jack needed a lift and in giving him one, Jack, in turn, lifted the spirits of a nation.

Watch video of Jack's run:
www.youtube.com/watch?v=_Jmisv1Spck

LESSON: By doing well for one, you can positively impact millions when compelling stories spread virally through digital and traditional media.

· · · · ·

"Surround yourself with only people who are going to lift you higher."

OPRAH WINFREY

· · · · ·

No. 35

Watch Your Language

- Have you ever said, "Man I wished I should have used foul language in my last post or used the f#$% word." No, but certainly the reverse is true...I wish I hadn't used that particular word. Words matter.

- Hateful words or phrases can be as damaging as obscene ones. If you wouldn't be comfortable wearing it as a T-shirt around the people that you reference, then do not post it online.

LEARNING MOMENTS

Six Nevada teenagers in middle school were arrested for posting and sending "Attack A Teacher Day."

One girl was arrested for sending the original post to over one hundred people and five others were arrested for responding with graphic details on which teacher they'd like to attack and what they would do to them.

The girls were surprised that they were subsequently arrested. They stated it was simply a joke.

"School shootings really happen. That's why we took it seriously. It's not OK, and it's not funny in this day and age if you're going to make a threat against a teacher," said Carson Middle School Principal, Dan Sadler.[53]

LESSON: Threats in digital context are no joking matter. Digital words matter.

No. 36

Teach & Train Your Team, Employees & Family

- When your employees, teammates or family members post something digitally, this will have a direct negative or positive reflection on them and you.

- Fool me once, shame on you; fool me twice, shame on me. When something negative occurs, you have nobody to blame but yourself, since you didn't take the time to teach and train your team, employees or family. A great first step is to give them this book. By helping others, you are ultimately helping yourself.

LEARNING MOMENTS

A Massachusetts high school teacher was fired for posting on Facebook, "I'm so not looking forward to another year at Cohasset Schools," she added that the community was "arrogant" and "snobby."

"I made a stupid mistake with my Facebook post, it may have cost me my career," she said.

LESSON: If you fail to train your teachers, employees or team how to use social media properly, it may result in you having to terminate an otherwise positive contributor.

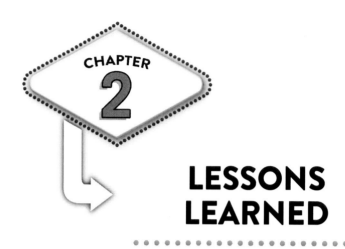

LESSONS LEARNED

Lessons Learned in Business & Hiring

CEO of Starbucks Learns Privacy is Dead

For example, Howard Schultz, while Chairman of Starbucks, was disturbed when an internal digital memo leaked out to the press, social networks and various blogs. Schultz approached his head of global communications, Wanda Herndon. "Did you hear about the memo?" asked Schultz. Wanda said yes, she knew about it. Schultz shook his head in disbelief and spoke about how hurt he was with the breach of trust. "Howard," Wanda said in the matter-of-fact way that Schultz had come to expect and appreciate from her, "Nothing is confidential. This is the new reality."

Schultz admitted as such, "The leaked memo helped me comprehend the enormous sea of change occurring in how information was flowing as well as what was being communicated. Technology was redefining the nature of relationships and how people spend their time. The fundamental societal shift was affecting the psyche of our own people and our customers. But not until the memo leaked did it affect me, and none too soon."[54]

LESSON: If one of the greatest CEOs of our time has identified a major shift and has taken steps to adjust how he leads, then maybe we all should.

• • • • •

Facebook CEO Posts Damage His Reputation

Facebook CEO Mark Zuckerberg has made some costly missteps as they relate to his reputation. Among them, he made negative comments to a friend that came across as conniving and backstabbing toward early developers of a Facebook-like social network.

> **Friend:** so have you decided what you are going to do about the websites?
>
> **Zuck:** yea i'm going to $%@k them

In another exchange leaked to Silicon Alley Insider, Zuckerberg explained to a friend that his control of Facebook gave him access to any information he wanted on any Harvard student:

> **Zuck:** yea so if you ever need info about anyone at harvard
>
> **Zuck:** just ask
>
> **Zuck:** i have over 4000 emails, pictures, addresses, sns
>
> **Friend:** what!? how'd you manage that one?
>
> **Zuck:** people just submitted it
>
> **Zuck:** i don't know why
>
> **Zuck:** they "trust me"4
>
> **Zuck:** dumb $%@ks

LESSON: If of the best technological minds in the world, Mark Zuckerberg, can make a digital mistake, then it can happen to anyone.

• • • • •

How an Unknown Company Gets the Best Talent

When Ed Nathanson became the lead of talent acquisition at Rapid7, he faced a challenge that many businesses face today.[55]

For hiring new employees, Rapid7 was completely dependent on external agencies. Ed had been given the difficult goal of hiring 100 top-notch employees annually. This was in one of the most competitive industries for talent: software security. Yet, Rapid7 didn't have coordination for hiring across the business lines and they were still tied to legacy job boards for talent. The recruiters at Rapid7 had a "post and pray" mentality.

Ed Nathanson was able to hire over 350 top-tier employees and:

- Achieved 493% LinkedIn follower growth in 2013
- Reduced time to fill from 100+ to 54 days
- Improved employee referrals from approximately 30% to 48%
- Was voted a "Top Place to Work" in 2011, 2012 and 2013 by the Boston Globe

With limited talent acquisition staff and fewer resources, how was this possible? This company also began with less than 500 employees.

The Key for Rapid7 was to focus on two things:

1. A "talent scout" recruiting model.

Ed understood that when you recruit someone new, you are selling a lifestyle change. Hence, he aligned his recruiters to business lines so that they "lived and breathed the goals and preferences of their hiring managers."

2. Be provocatively real.

Rapid7 had to compete with well-known brands in its industry. Hence, they took a different approach. They tried to reduce the number of people interested in their jobs by sending out edgy material via video cards, YouTube or LinkedIn. Nathanson stated, "Some people will see our video and say 'what the heck is that crap' and not apply. We think that's great. Because that means others will see it, LOVE it, and apply. We'll get better candidates for us."

Rapid7 also allowed employees to make fun homemade videos about a day-in-the-life at the company.

LESSON: Being authentic is a great weapon for small businesses to use against big companies when it comes to recruiting.

· · · · ·

Fitbit leaks sex stats to Google

Fitbit is a small chip used to help record your exercise activity—information that is then put into an online profile. One of the exercise activities included is sex. A problem arose when it was found that the privacy default setting on the online profiles was set to public. Therefore, when certain people's names were typed into Google's search box, a history of their sexual activity showed up through Fitbit. Making it worse was the fact that terms like "moderate effort" were often associated with the activity. [Source: *Digital Leader*]

· · · · ·

Chrysler flames Detroit drivers

Chrysler's social media agency accidentally sent this tweet on behalf of the auto company: "I find it ironic that Detroit is known as the #motorcity and yet no one here knows how to f$%#@ng drive." The agency employee that made the error—thinking he was sending via his personal account—

was fired that day. Chrysler also fired the agency. [Source: *Digital Leader*]

•••••

Kenneth Cole mistweets the Egyptians

Kenneth Cole: During the Egyptian Revolution, which was being aided by Twitter and Facebook, Kenneth Cole decided to tweet: "Millions are in uproar in #Cario. Rumor is they heard our new spring collection is now available online." Making light of a serious situation caused the company's pockets to be lighter as many protestors boycotted the clothing line. [Source: *Digital Leader*]

LESSON: As a CEO or leader of your organization your organization, your typing can help or harm future revenue.

•••••

Tim Armstrong AOL CEO fires
employee on conference call

Tim Armstrong, CEO of AOL, fired an employee during a conference call. Abel Lenz, Armstrong's Creative Director, reportedly tried to take a photo of Armstrong during the meeting concerning cutbacks. According to TechCrunch, a website owned by AOL, Armstrong said, "Abel, put that camera down. You're fired." Minutes later, Armstrong said, "The reason I fired Abel is I don't want anyone taking pictures of this meeting."

LESSON: Leaders need to understand they need to watch their words and actions as they are being broadcast. If Armstrong had to do it again, he probably would have said, "Abel, you are dismissed from this meeting." Then later, he could fire him.

Keith Kelly, "AOL'S Armstrong fires worker during conference call," New York Post, August 11, 2013, *www.nypost.com/ p/news/business/conference_gall_L7kFlZegr4EuO9QkSZUAgP*

· · · · ·

Carl Icahn tweet sends apple stock soaring

It's been called the "Tweet heard round the world." On August 13, 2013, Carl Icahn sent out a tweet that increased the stock price of Apple by 3% in minutes. His tweet read, "We currently have a large position in APPLE. We believe the company to be extremely undervalued. Spoke to Tim Cook today. More to come." [56]

Icahn has yet to disclose how much he invested in Apple, but CNBC reported his stake being worth over $2 billion. Almost immediately after the tweet, the stock's market capitalization increased $10 billion.

LESSON: Social media messages can have dynamic impacts on financial markets

· · · · ·

Woman fired before she's even hired

A young woman was happy to receive a job offer from Cisco. Not sure whether to take the job she posted on Twitter, "Cisco just offered me a job! Now I have to weigh the utility of a fatty paycheck against the daily commute to San Jose and hating the work." The company revoked the offer tweeting: "Who is the hiring manager? I'm sure they would love to know you will hate the work. We here at Cisco are versed in the Web."

LESSON: Saying negative comments about your current or future job has negative consequences.

· · · · ·

Twitter being used to cast movie stars

Twitter is now being used as a way to cast movies. President of global revenue at Twitter, Adam Bain, refers to it as a "Moneyball-style" approach to find actors. The actors are being considered because of their follower count as well as their engagement via social media with their fans.[57]

· · · · ·

From homeless to the broadcast booth

Ted Williams, a homeless man in Columbus, Ohio, become an Internet sensation after being approached by a *Dispatch* employee who saw and took a video on the side of the North Side highway holding a sign that read, "I have a God given gift of voice."[58] The reporter had him demonstrate his gift and uploaded it to Dispatch.com. After being posted to YouTube, the video has been viewed over 24.5 million times.

After just a couple of days, Williams was offered jobs from MTV, ESPN and the NFL (just to name a few). He has since worked doing voiceovers for companies such as Kraft Homestyle Macaroni and Cheese and the New England Cable News. He has also written a memoir telling his story. Just one simple YouTube video has changed this man's life forever. [59]

LESSON: Digital outlets can help discover unknown individuals and positively and dramatically change their life.

• • • • •

Billionaire Mark Cuban successfully defends his reputation

Billionaire businessman, Dallas Mavericks owner and Shark Tank star Mark Cuban was accused by the Securities and Exchange Commission (SEC) of insider trading. Cuban indicated, "The SEC took a flyer in 2006 on a case that had no foundation. They refused to drop the case. So we had to spend seven years and a lot of money to get to a point where a jury took just a few hours to confirm that the SEC did not have a case."

When asked on why he would be a target and be bullied by the SEC, Cuban responded, "Remember this dates back to 2006, when Linda Thomsen was the head of SEC enforcement. This is just my opinion, but I really get the sense that she had no idea what she was doing. She was looking for a name to prosecute, and I was the name she came upon. To give you a sense of timing, they announced the charges against me three weeks before Bernie Madoff was arrested. Maybe she knew Madoff was coming, and she wanted something to divert attention from it. What was certain was that they wanted the biggest bang for their public relations buck. Imagine how I felt to wake up the morning of November 18, 2008, and find that I was the non-stop headline (accused for something I didn't do). It wasn't fun. It made me sick to my stomach."

Even though it would have been easier to pay the fines, Cuban deemed it important to fight for his reputation. "I hate to be bullied. I love this country. The fact the SEC was ignoring facts and that they care only about winning rather than justice, just turned my stomach. I have the resources to fight. I felt compelled to take up that fight," said Cuban.

LESSON: Although it is often the most difficult road to take, you need to stand up and fight for your reputation.

· · · · ·

Costly photos

An NFL cheerleader was kicked off the New England Patriots Cheer Team after photos on Facebook showed her posing with a passed-out man whose body was covered in offensive and lewd felt marker drawings.

· · · · ·

Justin Bieber: From the streets to the Grammy's via YouTube

One of the most famous YouTube success stories is Justin Bieber. Throughout his tween years, his mother would post videos of Justin singing on YouTube. After a while, people took notice of this talented youngster. A Marketing Executive, Scooter Braun, then pursued Justin in hopes to represent him. At only 13 years old, Bieber recorded a demo and performed for hip-hop artist Usher who signed him to Raymond Braun Media Group.

Justin Bieber grew his net worth to $110 million and sold over 15 million albums and hundreds of sold out shows.[60] He is the most-followed person on Twitter with more followers then the populations of countries including Germany, Turkey, South Africa, Canada, Argentina and Egypt. Justin Bieber has YouTube (and his mother) to thank for all of this incredible fame and fortune.

· · · · ·

Lessons Learned: Personal & Family

Hands off my prom dress!

Teens are starting to use social media to alert their friends of their prom dress to help avoid another girl showing up wearing the same prom dress. Girls are immediately posting their purchased dresses via social outlets and telling others "don't you dare buy this same dress." It's essentially the modern day version of one marking their territory.

· · · · ·

Freshman suicide from cyberbullying

Phoebe Prince, a 15-year-old high school student from Massachusetts, was harassed by a group of "mean girls" for dating a senior within her first few weeks of her freshman year. Not only did they harass and threaten her at school, the girls would cyberbully her by calling her obscene names on Twitter, Craigslist, Facebook and Formspring.

Prince, unable to take the threats, went home from school and hung herself in a stairwell. Her bullies did not stop there; they continued to post mean comments on her Facebook memorial page. Seven teens were convicted of several crimes including: criminal harassment, stalking and civil rights violations.[61]

· · · · ·

Twitter helps during school shooting

During a school shooting at Lone Star College in Texas, students stuck inside the building were able to communicate with the outside world via Twitter. One student, Amanda, communicated a play by play of what she was experiencing including a tweet that read *"Everyone! There is a man shooting at Lonestar North Harris. This is not a joke. Please be safe. I'm so scared."* She was also able to contact a friend to tell her mother that she was safe. She was also contacted by CNN for more information and was sent well wishes from users located in Denmark.

Alex Fitzpatrick, "Student Tweets from Inside School during Shooting at Texas College" Mashable, January 22, 2013, mashable.com/2013/01/22/tweets-school-shooting/

· · · · ·

Don't text & drive!

After making the decision to text and drive, 20-something Jamie Nash, lost control of her car before ultimately being pinned inside the car as it caught fire. She was trapped in her burning car for over 20 minutes. Nash, a mother, was fortunate her kids weren't in the car.

She suffered third and fourth degree burns over the majority of her body. She required 30 surgeries in two years to treat the burns. Feeling fortunate to survive her horrific accident, she became determined to spread the word to stop texting and driving. She tells her story at schools and businesses in hopes to educate people on the risks of texting and driving. According the National Safety council, each year, 100,000 people crash while texting (U.S.).[62]

· · · · ·

Wrestler stands tall and inspires on Facebook

"He's always done everything; he hasn't let anything hold him back. He doesn't want to be different," says Anthony Robles' mother. Only her son is different, he's an NCAA wrestling champion. Few people have earned this title, and fewer still have done it on one leg—Anthony Robles was born without a right leg.

"I had a dream of playing football growing up, but I was too small for that so I decided on wrestling," says Robles. "I was a terrible wrestler, only about 90 pounds, but my mom told me God made me for a reason, and I believe that reason [God made me] is for wrestling."

Robles didn't see his condition as an obstacle. In fact, he has used it to his benefit. "It is a great advantage; my grip is extremely strong from walking on crutches all day using my hands and shoulders. My upper body strength is a huge advantage in my weight class."

He even ran his first mile on crutches in ten minutes and then reduced his time to eight minutes. "I think he has a goal of doing it in six minutes on crutches and, knowing Anthony, he'll accomplish it," said an Arizona State teammate.

In 2011, Robles completed a perfect senior season by winning his final wrestling match 7-1. "I wrestle because I love wrestling, but it inspires me when I get kids, even adults, who write me on Facebook or send me letters in the mail saying that I've inspired them, and they look up to me, and they're motivated to do things that other people wouldn't have thought possible." [Source: *Digital Leader* by Erik Qualman]

● ● ● ● ●

Welker's wife gone wild

After the AFC Championship game on January 20, 2013, Wes Welker's wife went on a Facebook rant after a frustrating loss. Anna Burns Welker posted a status that read,

"Proud of my husband and the Pats," Burns Welker wrote. "By the way, if anyone is bored, please go to Ray Lewis' Wikipedia page: 6 kids, 4 wives. Acquitted for murder. Paid a family off. Yay. What a hall of fame player! A true role model!"

She later apologized with a statement released to Larry Brown Sports. Burns Welker said, "I'm deeply sorry for my recent post on Facebook, I let the competitiveness of the game and the comments people were making about a team I dearly love get the best of me. My actions were emotional and irrational and I sincerely apologize to Ray Lewis and anyone affected by my comment after yesterday's game. It is such an accomplishment for any team to make it to the NFL playoffs, and the momentary frustration I felt should not overshadow the accomplishments of both of these amazing teams."[63]

LESSON: You represent your spouse, girlfriend, friends and family.

· · · · ·

Bus driver saves child from fall becomes YouTube star

Steven St. Bernard, a New York City bus driver, was arriving home from work when he heard some commotion. A seven-year-old autistic child had climbed out of a nearby apartment window and was dancing on top of an air conditioning unit several stories up.

Bernard prayed that if the girl jumped he would get there in time. The girl did jump and Bernard made it just in time to catch her fall. The girl suffered no injuries. Bernard tore a tendon in his hand. This unbelievable event was captured on YouTube.

"He has a heart, a very good heart—kids, adults, anybody— he would do anything for anybody," neighbor, Jessica Aleman, said of St. Bernard.[64]

LESSON: Social media can capture beautifully heroic acts. Remember that the eye in the sky never lies.

Watch incredible video: bit.ly/IjNlTG

· · · · ·

Billionaire bullied

T. Boone Pickens, billionaire and oilman, and three of his children are suing his son Michael Pickens in Dallas County Court for alleged cyberbullying and cyberstalking. They are suing him for five counts: invasion of privacy, defamation, libel, harmful access by computer and extortion. In 2012, Michael started a blog called "5 Days in Connecticut."

In the blog, he discussed his drug addiction and recovery. He then began to talk about how his addiction was due to his father's abuse, the drug addiction of his siblings and other personal family matters.

He tweeted and emailed links to the blog to people within the business. News stations then obtained the tweets. According to court documents, Boone and his three children say that Michael is lying in hopes to extort $20 million from Boone.[65] The family is asking for damages at the maximum lawful rate.

LESSON: Bullying happens in families, business, everywhere...

· · · · ·

You control how you react

"And if you don't give a damn what people think, they just don't bother disapproving. That's genuinely been my experience. I was talking to a friend yesterday about the opinions of others, and this extraordinary social media thing about which I obviously know nothing...it seems that people are incredibly vulnerable to what people are saying about them in these...what do they call them, social networks. It's pretty serious; we've had a couple of girls commit suicide over it. It is incomprehensible to me that anybody would pay the slightest bit of attention to what somebody had said about them on a computer."[66]

— *Dervla Murphy, 50-year veteran travel author*

· · · · ·

Jolly Green Giant stands tall against bullying

October is bully prevention month. Orange is the color worn to show support. As such, the famous 55-foot statue of the iconic Jolly Green Giant is often adorned with an orange toga in October.

LESSON: What's going to be your big stand?

· · · · ·

Twitter's ability to stop suicides

Health scientists at Brigham Young University have been researching the ability for Twitter to help prevent suicides by seeing warning signals. Their conclusion is that it can be an effective tool. The study indicates, "Twitter may be a viable tool for real-time monitoring of suicide risk factors on a large scale. Individuals who are at risk for suicide may be detected through social media." [67]

The researchers found that actually suicide rates mirror the rate of suicide chatter on Twitter, at the state level.

Health science professor at Brigham Young, Michael Barnes, believes, "The value of Twitter is that it is real time, and because it's real time, we have an opportunity to be taking action instead of looking at suicide data, suicide rates and saying 'What are we going to do?' If we can identify at-risk groups or populations, we're in a much better position to provide and intervention."[68]

LESSON: Social media, mobile and big data can be forces of good to prevent suicide.

· · · · ·

Twelve-year-old death the result of cyberbullying

Twelve-year-old Rebecca Sedwick leapt from atop a cement factory tower and plunged to her death. She was the victim of cyberbullying from 15 girls that ganged up on her online after she started dating a particular boy.

Sherriff Grady Judd was outraged stating, "I'm aggravated that the parents [of the bullies] aren't doing what parents should do. Responsible parents take disciplinary action. The parents do not think there is a problem here and that's a problem. One bullying suspect posted on Facebook: "Yes [I know] I bullied REBECCA and she killed herself but...I don't give a (expletive)."

Rebecca's mother sadly stated, "I can't say that I want these girls to spend the rest of their life in jail or any time in jail," she said, "but they do need serious rehabilitation."

LESSON: Parents need to take responsibility to ensure the set the right example for their kids and ensure they aren't bullies.

· · · · ·

Fifteen-year-old mentors cyberbullying victims

Natalie Farzaneh, a high school student, became a victim of cyberbullying after getting a Facebook and Formspring account. Through these social media accounts, people would message her telling her to commit suicide and that the world would be better off without her. These messages led her to suicidal thoughts and ultimately self-harming.

Farzaneh turned her abuse into a way to work as an advocate for surviving these cyber-bullies. As a 15-year-old, she works as a mentor for the beat bullying program called Cyber Mentoring. She also works as a motivational speaker for different schools.

Paige Chandler, a cyberbullying victim, was attacked via Formspring. People would send her anonymous comments insulting her appearance calling her "ugly and fat."

At the age of 17, she also has joined CyberMentor.org.uk to help other victims of online abuse.[69]

LESSON: Anyone, old and young, can stand up and fight evil.

· · · · ·

The greatness of a man is not in how much wealth he acquires, but in his integrity and his ability to affect those around him positively.

BOB MARLEY

· · · · ·

Lessons Learned in Teams & Athletics

No Super Bowl for you

NFL referee Brian Stopolo was relieved of his duties prior to a New Orleans Saints football game. Stopolo's Facebook page revealed that he was a Saints fanatic. The page included photos of Stopolo in full Saints gear and enjoying tailgates at Saints games. One post said "That's awesome you get to be an official for a Saints game! I didn't think they would let you since you're from Louisiana."

The NFL played it safe and removed him from the game so as not to risk the appearance of impropriety.

• • • • •

Costly $370 per character tweet for Mark Cuban

Following a tough basketball game loss, Dallas Mavericks owner was fined $50,000, or nearly $370 per character, for posting to Twitter: "Im sorry NBA fans. Ive tried for 13 yrs to fix the officiating in this league and I have failed miserable. Any Suggestions? I need help"

• • • • •

Half a million dollar fine

During the course of the 2011 NBA lockout, many angry fans were upset with the owners. Miami Heat owner tweeted "Honestly you are barking at the wrong owner," implying he wasn't for the lockout.

As this was viewed as a public break in solidarity amongst the owners, Arson was fined $500,000 by the league commissioner.

· · · · ·

Prince's debauchery in Vegas

England's Prince Harry had a wild night in Las Vegas, which entailed him playing a game of strip billiards and challenging Olympic gold medal swimmer Ryan Lochte to a race in the hotel pool.

Later that evening, photos were taken of a drunk Harry playing naked air guitar and making out with a British blonde. These offline antics did not stay in Vegas as images were posted online and videos of the debauchery were uploaded to YouTube.

· · · · ·

Secret Service bored

A member of the Secret Service mistakenly thought he was posting to his own Twitter account, but instead his disapproval of Fox News went out on behalf of the entire secret service: "Had to monitor Fox for a story. Can't. Deal. With. The. Blathering."

· · · · ·

LEARNING MOMENT

San Francisco 49ers quarterback Colin Kaepernick "favorites" all the negative tweets that are posted about him. Before every game, he reads some of these negative posts and it motivates him to prove his detractors wrong.

LESSON: Turn negative or critical posts into positive motivation.

· · · · ·

Famous celebrity embarrassed by mum's tweets

Andy Murray, a world-ranked British tennis star, was embarrassed by his mother's tweet at Wimbledon. It used to be that your mom could only embarrass you by cheering to loud. But, when Judy Murray tweeted about Murray's opponent, Feliciano Lopez of Spain, "Oooooooooh Delicaino....looking good out there. As always," it took embarrassment to a completely new level.

LESSON: What you post can have ramifications on your children's future, so act like an adult...a mature adult.

· · · · ·

Teen jailed for video game threats

Justin Carter (18) was arrested and put behind bars for a Facebook post. He was charged after playing the video game League of Legends and engaging in an online conversation with another player he was competing against. Carter posted on Facebook: I'm f**ed in the head alright. I'ma shoot up a kindergarten. And watch the blood of the innocent rain down. And eat the beating heart of one of them."

Additional probes showed Carter was also engaged in online bullying. He could serve up to eight years in jail.

LESSON: Avoid sarcasm, especially around threats and violence. Do not give authorities a chance to misinterpret items; it's not worth the penalty. All digital evidence will be used either for or against your case.

· · · · ·

Video helps man get recruited by Harlem Globetrotters

After posting a video onto YouTube, Jacob Tucker became famous. As an Illinois College basketball player, Tucker used the video of himself doing slam dunks as an audition for the college slam dunk championship contest. After winning an online fan vote on Facebook, he filled the final spot. The video was viewed over 3.1 million times. Tucker ended up winning the dunk contest and has since been recruited by the Harlem Globetrotters.[70]

LESSON: One reason to use social media and mobile tools is so that the world can discover your talent.

· · · · ·

Jay Bilas catches NCAA in hypocrisy

ESPN college basketball analyst, Jay Bilas, unveiled the hypocrisy in the selling of individual jerseys and team memorabilia on NCAA's website through Twitter. After exposing the results of the NCAA site's search, they disabled the function. Mark Emmert, NCAA president, said, "In the national office, we can certainly recognize why that could be seen as hypocritical, and indeed I think the business of having the NCAA selling those kinds of goods is a mistake, and we're going to exit that business immediately. It's not something that's core to what the NCAA is about, and it probably never should have been in the business."

NCAA is involved with quite a few lawsuits for using the names of college athletes for personal gain and no compensation for the athletes.[71]

LESSON: Even algorithms of organizations are being held accountable, because someone (e.g., executive) signed off on the implementation.

· · · · ·

Eagles wide receiver Riley Cooper uses N-word

Riley Cooper, Eagles wide receiver, dropped the N-word at a Kenny Chesney concert at Lincoln Financial Field. The confrontation was captured on video. In the video, Cooper says "I will jump that fence and fight every n***** here, bro." He then tweeted, "I am so ashamed and disgusted with myself. I want to apologize. I have been offensive. I have apologized to my coach, Jeffrey Lurie, Howie Roseman and to my teammates. I owe an apology to the fans and to this community. I am so ashamed, but there are no excuses. What I did was wrong and I will accept the consequences." Owner Jeffrey Lurie released a statement saying that he Cooper was fined for the incident.[72]

LESSON: Excessive drinking can get you into more trouble than ever before. Getting drunk is a much more dangerous proposition than it was a decade ago, especially if you become loose with your words or actions.

· · · · ·

Ohio State fan names his cancer Michigan.
Beat Michigan.

Twelve-year-old Grant Reed from Ohio named his cancer "Michigan" in order to keep his spirits up after being diagnosed with brain cancer in 2011. He has beat Michigan and is currently in remission. After his story went nationwide, he has gotten a hospital visit from the Buckeyes' head coach Urban Meyer. He also got a call from Michigan head coach Brady Hoke inviting him and his family to the Ohio State-Michigan game. Grant's father, Troy, stated, "It's getting hard to keep my dislike for them, because they've been so classy and unbelievable to us."[73]

LESSON: Sometimes the person that seems like the enemy in a story can actually be the hero. Do not make assumptions.

· · · · ·

Roddy White's emotional tweets get the better of him

After George Zimmerman was found not guilty for the death of Trayvon Martin, Atlanta Falcons receiver Roddy White went to twitter to react to the verdict. Many athletes took to Twitter to voice their opinions, but White's took a turn for the worst.

He tweeted, "All them jurors should go home tonight and kill themselves for letting a grown man get away with killing a kid."

That Sunday, he tweeted an apology saying, "I understand my tweet last nite [*sic*] was extreme. I never meant for the people to do that. I was shocked and upset about the verdict. I am sorry."[74]

LESSON: Measure your words twice and post once, especially when it involves an emotional topic.

· · · · ·

Golfer Lee Westwood rants online after hours

Lee Westwood went on a Twitter rant expressing his frustrations with being 13 shots behind the winner Jason Dufner at the PGA Championships. Tweets included:

"Come on you girly boy trolls! I've only won just over 2 mill on course this year! Need you to keep me entertained a bit longer than this!"

"If you're going to abuse me at least do it properly! Numbskulls!"

"Yes only got to the best in the WORLD! Is that your boy band in that pic!? Ooo er missus!"

He then tweeted an apology stating, "Sincere apologies to my sponsors and true followers for my earlier comments. It was out of order and out of character, Westy."[75]

LESSON: Nothing good happens after midnight offline or online.

· · · · ·

Even 310-pound football players can be bullied

Jonathon Martin was a starting player for the Miami Dolphins when he suddenly left the team. His lawyer indicated his reason for departure was the result of bullying from his teammates and one teammate in particular, Richie Incognito.

While this story is in its infancy at the writing of this book, there is still much to be learned from it. What's interesting is this incident involving two grown men (both over 300 pounds) exhibits some of the standard traits of teenage bullying.

1. Victim is blamed; many blamed Martin for not standing up for himself.

2. Poor advice and leadership from people that should know better (the General Manager told Martin's agent that Martin should just simply punch Incognito in the face).

LESSON: Bullying and hazing occurs beyond the middle school playground. If it can happen in the National Football League, then it can happen in your business or organization.

● ● ● ● ●

Lessons Learned in Crime & Politics

UK man jailed for sarcastic threats against airport

Paul Chambers, a UK based tax accountant, was planning to fly out of Robin Airport. To his disappointment, he discovered the airport was closed and his flight cancelled. An avid Twitter user, Chambers immediately posted:

> "Robin Hood airport is closed. You've got a week and a bit to get your **** together otherwise I'm blowing the airport sky high!"

While Chambers later indicated he was satirically messing around, a Robin Airport employee didn't find it such a laughing matter. He immediately alerted the authorities about Chambers' post. Chambers was apprehended by police at his office, was convicted and fined 3,000 British Pounds for a post deemed "menacing" in its content. Chambers also lost his job.

LESSON: Joking about terrorist attacks either offline or online is no laughing matter and can have serious consequences.

· · · · ·

Digital deputies

Looters and rioters in Vancouver following Game 7 of the 2011 Stanley Cup Finals learned a tough lesson. Photos and video posted online helped police conduct "Facebook justice" and arrest hundreds of violators. Many of these citizens not only received criminal punishment, but also subsequently lost their jobs. Unlike in the offline world where there may only be a handful of eyewitnesses, online there are millions of digital deputies.

· · · · ·

Silk Road shutdown:
Site that sold heroin & hit men shutdown

Silk Road, a nefarious site that sold everything from heroin to murder, was eventually discovered and shut down. FBI agent Christopher Tarbell said, "The site succeeded to make conducting illegal transactions on the Internet as easy and frictionless as shopping online at mainstream e-commerce websites."[76]

Founder, Ross Ulbricht (29), used a complex system underground network "onion router" or "thor" to bounce encrypted message across various machines globally. This makes it incredibly difficult to track to origin of messages and transactions. As a result, Silk Road was able to develop a billion dollar business.

Authorities eventually caught Ulbricht when he posted, using his own name, a question on a public message board seeking assistance for a complex coding issue around Silk Road.

LESSON: No matter how technically savvy you are at hiding things...there is always someone better at uncovering them.

· · · · ·

Texting teen sentenced for 15 years

A Massachusetts teenager was condemned to prison and lost his license for 15 years for causing a fatal crash. His mobile data usage showed he was texting when the accident occurred. This was used in the court of law to help convict him.[77]

LESSON: Texting and driving kills. Your mobile data can and will be used in a court of law.

• • • • •

What's on your phone can and will be used against you

Boston police arrested Brima Wurie on a minor charge and confiscated his phone. They then noticed an unusual amount of calls coming in from a known drug house and as a result were able to book him later on drug dealing.

San Diego police pulled over David Riley for having expired tags. Pictures on Riley's phone incriminated Riley as being part of a gang shooting in 2009.

LESSON: There is an ongoing legal debate about privacy (Fourth Amendment), mobile devices and their use in the legal system, but mobile phones and what's on them can often be used against you in the court of law.[78]

• • • • •

Confessing drunk driving manslaughter on YouTube

Matthew Cordle admitted in a YouTube video that he was responsible for killing a man via drinking and driving. In it, Cordle explains, "This video will act as my confession. When I get charged, I will plead guilty and take full responsibility for everything I've done to Vincent and his family. I won't dishonor Vincent's memory by lying about what happened." Cordle dismissed attorney's advice to lie and that his Breathalyzer test could be thrown out of court. "All I would have to do is lie," Cordle stated, "I won't go down that path." [79]

LESSON: The world is radically different than it was a decade ago.

• • • • •

Losing a presidency

While running for president, Mitt Romney discovered how nothing is confidential. Romney made some ill-advised comments at a private fundraising event. What Romney failed to realize is he was being secretly video recorded. His famous "47% line" went like this:

> *"All right, there are 47% who are with him (President Obama), who are dependent upon government, who believe that they are victims, who believe the government has a responsibility to care for them ... And they will vote for this president no matter what ... These are people who pay no income tax ... My job is not to worry about those people. I'll never convince them they should take personal responsibility and care for their lives."*

LESSON: We need to realize that we always have to "be on message" as there is no such thing anymore as "behind closed doors."

• • • • •

Hit & post

18-year-old Jacob Cox-Brown was arrested by Astoria (Oregon) police nine hours after posting "Drivin drunk ... classsic ;) but to whoever's vehicle i hit i am sorry. :P" [80]

Two people digitally connected Cox-Brown's sent messages to the Astoria police alerting them. This clue was vital in the police linking Cox-Brown to a 1 a.m. hit and run involving two other parked vehicles. Without the post, the police most likely would not have solved this particular hit-and-run incident.

• • • • •

Naked profile pictures exposed

Joseph Bernard Campbell was charged with hacking into 19 different women's Facebook accounts and stealing nude or semi-nude photos of the women. Later, he hacked into the accounts and posted these pilfered photos as their main profile picture.

Campbell indicated that he knew most of the women and his intent was "to harass the victims and cause them emotional distress." [81]

Many of the photos that Campbell stole were private photos sent from women, via Facebook, to their fiancés serving overseas in the military.

Campbell pleaded guilty to charges of cyberstalking and unauthorized access to a computer. Each of these crimes has a maximum penalty of five years in federal prison along with a $250,000 fine.

● ● ● ● ●

Murder for hire

London Eley digitally posted about her ex-boyfriend and father of her child, Corey White, "I will pay somebody a stack to kill my baby father." "Baby father" is in reference to White and a "stack" is slang for $1,000.

Timothy Bynum responded with, "Say no more ... what he look like ... where he be at ... need that stack 1st." (*sic*)

Eley and Bynum were arrested and charged with attempted murder. White was killed a few months later. Authorities weren't certain if the posts were linked to his death.

● ● ● ● ●

NOTE: Digital resources listed
are free for users unless
noted otherwise.

TOP 15 DIGITAL
REPUTATION TOOLS

Brand Yourself

Brand Yourself puts the power of reputation management in your own hands by providing tools for a do-it-yourself digital reputation audit. Users can actively improve their own Google results. Key features include the ability for users to submit links they would like to appear when someone searches their name on Google, the ability to track your progress via emailed custom alerts, and the ability to send notifications when your name is Googled.

brandyourself.com

Buffer

Buffer is a free tool that shares your content across the web at the best possible times throughout the day so that your followers and fans see your updates more frequently.

bufferapp.com

Buzz Bundle

Buzz Bundle is a service that provides social media management tools to handle all your social media and reputation management activities. Companies and individuals can use Buzz Bundle for posting, responding and joining conversations on a variety of social media outlets. (Cost: $199)

www.buzzbundle.com

Epic Browser

Epic Browser is a web browser that aims to improve user privacy by defaulting to private browsing mode thus preventing the recording of history, caches, passwords and other features that may reveal information about the user. Key features include private browsing as well as the ability to clear all browsing data automatically once your session is complete.

www.epicbrowser.com

Google Alerts

Google Alerts are email updates of the latest relevant Google results (web, news, etc.) based on your queries. You may choose to set up a Google Alert for your name, business or organization as a way to monitor your digital reputation. You can control the number and frequency of the alerts as well as the email address to which the alerts are connected. Most of us should use this to track our name and the name of our organization.

www.google.com/alerts

Google Analytics

Google Analytics is a tool offered by Google that not only provides extensive data about a website's traffic and traffic sources but also measures conversions and sales. When monitoring your digital reputation, Google Analytics can provide vital information about web traffic that will help you become more strategic. It can also tell you the demographics of people who visit your pages.

www.google.com/analytics

Hootsuite

Hootsuite is a free tool that allows you to monitor activity on all social networks easily. You may choose to monitor all tweets that include your name or the name of your company, product or organization. Hootsuite pulls all keywords that you want tracked into one easy to read column. Popular features include the ability to post one message to all your social networks simultaneously, an ability to store your favorite posts, and the opportunity to pre-schedule social media posts.

hootsuite.com/features/mobile-apps/iphone

≡ (No. 8) ≡

Klout

Klout is a website and mobile app designed to measure online social influence using an algorithm that analyzes a user's social media platforms in terms of size and engagement. A Klout score is one way that you or, or your brand can reach across platforms and measure key reputation components including influence. Popular features include the Klout score, an ability to score your digital influence as well as a list of topics, which describe your influence within your network. The scores range from 0-100, with 100 the best.

Movie producers often use Klout when they launch a movie premiere in a new city. For example, if a new movie, starring Selma Hayek, is set to premiere in Miami than the producers would have Klout send a message to all Miami area users who have a Klout score of 80 or above in terms of movie influence. The user would receive an invitation to attend the movie premiere and meet Selma Hayek. The guests would arrive, enjoy their premiere experience and post items to their digital followers.

During Fashion Week in New York, some of the exclusive parties only allowed access to individuals who possessed a Klout score of 70 or higher.

klout.com/home

Kred

Similar to Klout, Kred is a tool designed to measure influence. Kred is unique because it is the first and only influence measuring tool to publicly share the algorithm they use to identify a user's score. Kred can help you or your brand measure influence within a specific community of interest. Popular features include the ability to view leading influencers within a specific digital community, a transparent process and algorithm for measuring influence, and a detailed monthly reporting of engagement and outreach.

kred.com

LinkedIn

LinkedIn is the number one social platform for developing a professional network, finding new job opportunities and building a digital reputation. Users should complete their profile in its entirety. The reason? According to LinkedIn, a complete LinkedIn profile receives 40 times more opportunities than an incomplete profile. Key features of LinkedIn include the ability to connect with professionals in every industry, search and filtering features, ability to create a detailed professional profile others can search and excellent job boards.

www.linkedin.com/

= (No. 11) =

Reputation Alert (iOS)

Reputation Alert is an iOS mobile app that monitors keywords on Twitter. Users can set names, brands, organizations or specific product names as keywords and monitor any Twitter mentions. (Cost: $0.99)

itunes.apple.com/us/app/reputation-alert/id493065518?mt=8

= (No. 12) =

Socialmention.com

Socialmention.com is a search tool specifically designed to search social networking sites. This tool monitors one's presence across various social media platforms. Popular features include filterable results, sentiment analysis reporting, listing of top hashtags (#), as well as users associated with each search query.

socialmention.com

= (No. 13) =

Trendpedia

Trendpedia is a blog search tool that compares up to three searches simultaneously. Your brand can see how often a product name was mentioned in comparison to a competitor's product. Key features include comparison searching, keyword searches on social media and blogging sites, and visualization of the results.

www.trendpedia.com

Vizify

Vizify is a site that helps transform the interesting impressions you make online into one definitive, multidimensional, graphic biography. Vizify biographies can be used not only as a personal website but also as an online profile and an email signature. Key features include the ability to pull highlights from a variety of online channels, a beautiful sleek design and an easy to use format. The sophisticated, creative results belie the simplicity of the website.

www.vizify.com

WhosTalkin

WhosTalkin is branded as a blog search tool. This sophisticated tool allows users to search for conversations surrounding topics they most value. The site has a simple design that allows the user to search across blogs, major news sites, social media networks and much more. It provides brands and individuals with comprehensive reporting of keyword mentions in order to monitor reputation effectively.

www.whostalkin.com

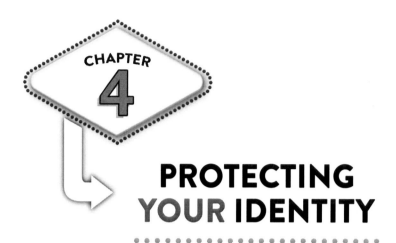

PROTECTING YOUR IDENTITY

Identity theft is the fastest growing crime in the United States. Criminals use information from our social networks to poach our identity. Below are 20 tips to help prevent you from becoming a victim.

20 Tactical Tips to Protect Your Identity

≡ (No. 1) ≡

Be careful with under the door menus

Whether you are in a hotel or your own home, be wary of menus slipped under your door Identity thieves often use these fake menus to capture your personal and credit card information when you call the restaurant. To assure your safety, go online or contact the hotel's front desk to place an order.

≡ (No. 2) ≡

Your Smartphone is vulnerable

Make sure your computers, mobile devices and wearable technology have the latest security software. Frequently update this software.

≡ ⟨*No.* **3**⟩ ≡

Do not use public Wi-Fi for financial transactions

If you are using public Wi-Fi in a hotel or restaurant, do not go online for banking, stock trades or other important financial matters. Perform these transactions in the safety of your home. Similarly, do not use publicly shared computers for such transactions. For example, if you are in the library, do not access your investment account. Identity thieves have "keylogging" software on these machines, which track everything you push on the keyboard.

≡ ⟨*No.* **4**⟩ ≡

Beware of free Wi-Fi

Identify thieves often name Wi-Fi hotspots as official connections for various locations, including hotels, airports or restaurants. For example, the hotspot might be named "freewifi" or "hotelwifi." If you use these unsecured networks, you are at risk. If you are uncertain which is the correct Wi-Fi, simply ask an airport official, desk clerk or waitress.

≡ ⟨*No.* **5**⟩ ≡

Avoid phishing scams

Should you receive solicitations from companies, banks or other organizations, do not click on the links. It is much safer to go directly to the home pages of these sites to find the specific offer or issue. If you choose to click through, make certain that the URL is correct. Example: *www.bankofamerica.com* not *bankofamerica.randomsite.com.* Phishers develop fake company web pages and fake company emails presenting themselves as reputable companies. The phishers are now in position to steal your password and personal information.

Be very suspicious of requests for your personal information from anyone including your email provider. Triple-check to ensure the request is legitimate before taking any action. Your email provider will rarely send you a message, so be alert when you receive one and make sure it is not a phishing scam.

$$\equiv \left(\begin{array}{c} \textit{No.} \\ \textbf{6} \end{array}\right) \equiv$$

Set up a password for online card use

Do not post important personal information on social networks. Choose personal security questions that cannot be answered by your Facebook information.

$$\equiv \left(\begin{array}{c} \textit{No.} \\ \textbf{7} \end{array}\right) \equiv$$

Be careful on online auctions, such as eBay

Pay the seller directly with a credit card so you can dispute the charges if the merchandise does not arrive or is misrepresented. Whenever possible, avoid paying by check or money order.

$$\equiv \left(\begin{array}{c} \textit{No.} \\ \textbf{8} \end{array}\right) \equiv$$

Destroy digital data

When you sell, trade or dispose of a computer system, a hard drive, a recordable CD, backup tape or DVD, you must take precautions to ensure the data is completely and irrevocably destroyed. Deleting the data or reformatting the hard drive is insufficient. Anyone with technological savvy can undelete files or recover data from a formatted drive. Use a product like *ShredXP* to ensure that data on hard drives is completely destroyed. Physically destroy CD, DVD or tape media by breaking or shattering before disposal or use shredders that are specifically designed for this purpose.

$$\equiv \left(\begin{array}{c} cNo. \\ 9 \end{array}\right) \equiv$$

Use strong passwords for all online accounts

Use a strong password that includes symbols, numbers and upper and lower case letters to protect your identity. If you have a hard time making up a strong password, try using a mnemonic device. For example, "I was born at New York Mercy Hospital in 1975" becomes "Iwb@NYMHi1975." Vary your passwords because thieves have easier access to your personal information when you use the same password for each account.

$$\equiv \left(\begin{array}{c} cNo. \\ 10 \end{array}\right) \equiv$$

Limit the personal information you share online

The number of available social networks increases daily and your personal information is available to anyone. Protect yourself from identity thieves by not posting personal information, especially your address, phone numbers, SSN, birth date or birthplace.

• • • • •

I would rather go to any extreme than suffer anything that is unworthy of my reputation, or of that of my crown.

ELIZABETH I

• • • • •

№ 11

Be careful when shopping online

Use secure sites when shopping online and research unfamiliar sites to ensure they are real. When checking the security of the website, look for https://. The "s" that is displayed after "http" indicates the website is secure. The "s" is occasionally invisible until you move to the order page. Thieves use shopping websites to collect credit card numbers and other private information.

№ 12

Confirmation of order

Once your online purchase is complete, you will receive a confirmation page that summarizes your order and includes your customer information, product information and confirmation number. Print one copy of the confirmation page as well as the page delineating company name, postal address, phone number and legal terms, including return policy. Keep these for your own records for the period covered by the return/warranty policy. The merchant may also email a confirmation message. Save and/or print that message as well as any other company correspondence.

№ 13

Keep track of personal information

Do not carry your extra credit cards, social security card, birth certificate or passport in your wallet or purse unless absolutely necessary. This practice minimizes the information a thief can steal.

≡ 14 ≡

Check your credit report

Order a copy of your credit report periodically to ensure your information is accurate and includes only those activities you authorized. When you require credit to buy a home or obtain a credit card, unresolved issues will not stand in the way of a successful outcome.

≡ 15 ≡

Destroy hotel key cards

Hotel magnetic key cards contain all the personal information you provided to the front desk staff. Cut the cards in half and destroy them.

≡ 16 ≡

Ask for credit card verification

Your signature on the back of your credit card validates the card and expresses agreement with the banks' terms. When you place "SEE ID" on the card, you inform the clerks to check the name and signature on the card against a driver's license.

≡ 17 ≡

Sign out

Website logins have added a "stay signed in" or "keep me signed in" check box. Do not use this option! *Always* uncheck this box, especially when using a shared computer. This option appears convenient, but checking "stay signed in" to your account allows hackers to access your personal information easily.

≡ (*No.* **18**) ≡

Be aware of your surroundings

Criminals can access your personal information quickly and easily, through their camera phones. Therefore, be wary of people standing extremely close to you when you are using your debit or credit card. Make every effort to use the same ATM so you can tell when the equipment looks different. When entering your PIN number in an ATM, position your body so others cannot see the keys you are pressing.

Close all unused credit card accounts and bank accounts.

≡ (*No.* **19**) ≡

Keep copies of cards and documents

Keep copies of all your identification cards, credit cards and other important documents. You now have the 1-800 phone numbers and account numbers to contact the credit card company in the event your card is lost or stolen.

≡ (*No.* **20**) ≡

Treat mail with care

Always deposit outgoing mail containing personally identifying information in a post office collection box or at the post office rather than an unsecured mailbox and collect your mail daily. Consider a switch to paperless billing by contacting our bank, credit card provider or other companies from whom you receive mailed bills. Contact the United States Postal Service to request a vacation hold if you plan to be away from home and no one is available to pick up your mail. The United States Postal Service will hold your mail at your local post office for a select period of time until you can pick it up.

● ● ● ● ●

"The task of the modern educator is not to cut down jungles, but to irrigate deserts."

C. S. LEWIS

● ● ● ● ●

PUTTING YOUR BEST FACE FORWARD

20 Tips to be a Video Star

It's estimated by 2017 that over 60 percent of the content we consume on our mobile devices will be video content. As such, all of us will be on video, whether it is simply for a conversation with the family via video or if we are being interviewed by a national media outlet.

Since these videos will be archived forever, it is important for us to put our best face forward. Below are 20 tips to help you look like a professional.

Relax your face

This actually starts with the rest of your body. Make sure your hands aren't balled up and your shoulders aren't scrunched. Some people find it helpful to give a little self-massage on the temple and neck. Also, rubbing your palms together to generate warmth and placing them onto your closed eyes is another trick to help relax your face.

Smile

Specifically concentrate on raising your cheekbones. This will naturally give the illusion to the camera that your eyes are sparkling.

Focus on yoga-esque breaths

Deep and slow. This breathing technique will help relax your face and body and also will help prevent you from talking too fast.

Nixe the non-verbals

If being interviewed do not use normal non-verbal cues like nodding your head. This is different from a normal conversion. If you nod, it appears as if you are a "know it all" and are impatient for the question. It conveys to the audience that you already know the answer. This is a difficult habit to break so you may not get it right the first few times you are on camera; but with a little practice, it will become second nature.

Mic it up

When possible use a good microphone; they are cheap, so go out and buy a good one.

≡ (No. 6) ≡

Lighting to look your best

Make sure the light is in your face and not behind you. Natural light is best at dawn and dusk. If you can shoot during these periods, it will make you look your best.

≡ (No. 7) ≡

Have good posture

Stand up against a wall and have your shoulders and the top of the back of your head pressed firmly against the wall and slowly walk away from the wall keeping this posture intact for the camera; feel free to go back to slouching once the lights go off!

≡ (No. 8) ≡

Overemphasize everything

Overemphasize your words, excitement, volume, gestures, eyes, etc. Do not shout as if you are scolding a misbehaving dog (see #2 about being relaxed), but you need to project as if you are on stage performing a play. The first time I saw Magic Johnson being interviewed, I thought why is he shouting instead of talking in his normal voice? Then I found out the first few times I saw myself interviewed—if you are talking in your normal tone, you come across as drab and unexcited. If the bubbly Magic Johnson has to take it up a notch to look excited on film, then we all need to!

Be concise

If you are filming your own video, make it less than two minutes. If you are being interviewed, answer the question with your most powerful statement first. If it appears, the interviewer wants more than you can go to the second and third most powerful points.

Sit on your tails

If you are wearing a suit jacket, tuck the tails of your coat under your behind and place your sitting bones firmly on them. This will give a nice line on your shoulders.

Make-up

If offered HD make-up, accept it. I know this will be tough for guys at first; but if you do not have it you can look tired, shiny and old on HD. If you are at home, apply base make-up with a brush—this will dramatically reduce shine and lines. If you are like me and do not have base make-up lying around, use a cotton swap to go over your face quickly to at least remove the oil and dirt.

No. 12

Hydrate

Make sure to drink plenty of fluids beforehand. Have water nearby in case you need it. Avoid ice and sugary drinks. Sparkling water with lemon is the best.

No. 13

The camera is your audience

Spend the majority of the time looking into the camera. The camera is your audience. If you are on Skype/Facetime, do not watch your little image in the corner. Look into the camera. If you are being interviewed, ask the interviewer where you should place most of your eye contact. When you get on the television show *Ellen*, make sure you know where the various cameras are and "work" each camera. If speaking on stage and you are being recorded, ask the cinematographer where you can and can't walk to be in the light and in the frame still. Make sure you play to the camera for your major points of emphasis; you can use these for your highlight reel later.

No. 14

Hum happy birthday

Before you begin speaking, a good trick is to hum happy birthday and then immediately say, "The rain in Spain falls mainly on the plain."

☰ ⑮ ☰

Comfortable Clothes

Wear clothes that you are most comfortable in—what you feel you look the best in, but do not have things that would distract [e.g. large broach, crazy tie, dress with a puffy/flowery design near the top]. If you are comfortable, then you will be confident. For David Cameron, this might be a suite with a blue tie; for Garth Brooks, it might be jeans and an open collared black shirt. Try to be consistent in what you wear on video; this makes you more memorable. Johnny Cash—the man in black, Tiger Woods—red shirt on Sundays, Gene Simmons—exercise tank top, Mark Zuckerberg—hooded sweatshirt, etc.

☰ ⑯ ☰

Soothing your throat

If you feel like you have a frog in your throat, eat some cantaloupe, as this provides soothing lubrication.

☰ ⑰ ☰

Be Yourself

The above are tips to help put your best face forward. Make sure you are yourself on the camera. This can be difficult. Some speaking coaches say do not use your hands, but then I paid close attention to one of the best speakers in the world, Jim Collins (author of *From Good to Great*) and he definitely uses his hands. The difference was that every movement had a purpose. Hence, the use of his hands assisted his delivery rather than distract from the message. If you are going to move, move with a purpose. If you are used to speaking with your hands, then speak with your hands. If you speak with your hands, then try to make sure you raise them up so that they are in frame of the camera; the worst thing is for a finger to be occasionally flying in and out of frame. If the video is only showing your head, then try to lower your hands so they have less of a chance to fly into the frame randomly. Never have your hands block your face unless you are demonstrating being ashamed.

$$= \left(\text{No. } 18 \right) =$$

Pay it forward

Do the courtesy of all the above when filming someone else. Make them a star and they will shine brightly on you!

$$= \left(\text{No. } 19 \right) =$$

Have Fun!

$$= \left(\text{No. } 20 \right) =$$

Do post-mortems.

The beautiful thing about video is you can review. Act as if you are the head coach of the New England Patriots and review video to get an advantage. How many "um"s do you say, are you slouching, do you look better with your glasses on or off, do you say "like" or other "pet" words too often. What little quirks do you have (dropping your head, slouching your shoulders, turning your back to the audience, shifty eyes)? Review these and put them into the notes section of your phone.

Review the top three quirks you have the night before giving a presentation and right before you go on stage, as this will remind you to work on them.

Some of the best you can learn from: Benjamin Zander, Dan Heath, Jim Collins, Tim Sanders, Guy Kawasaki, Andy Stanley.

• • • • •

Think about what people are doing on Facebook today. They're keeping up with their friends and family, but they're also building an image and identity for themselves, which in a sense is their brand. They're connecting with the audience that they want to connect to. It's almost a disadvantage if you're not on it now.

MARK ZUCKERBERG

• • • • •

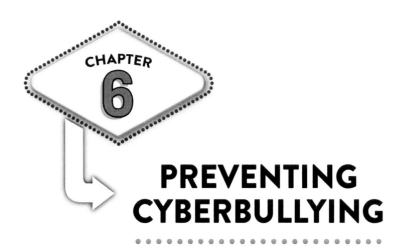

PREVENTING CYBERBULLYING

14 Ways to Prevent and Stop Cyberbullying

(1) Do not communicate with cyberbullies.

(2) Notify the abuser's online service.

(3) Search online to ensure there are no photos or compromising personal information, which could be used against you.

(4) Think twice before posting anything that could hurt someone's reputation.

(5) Do not put anything online that other people might find offensive.

(6) Encourage your children to seek help from an adult whenever they feel threatened.

(7) Never share your password.

(8) Log off all online accounts, especially accounts on public computers.

(9) Set your privacy settings.

(10) If you witness bullying, tell the offender to stop; hurtful behavior is unacceptable.

(11) Activities that are illegal offline are often illegal online.

(12) When you witness bullying and choose to ignore that behavior, your silence implies acceptance. Be an "upstander," not a bystander.

(13) Do not send messages when you are angry.

(14) Do not be a cyberbully. Model appropriate behavior.

Your voice does matter. In England in a four-year span, cyber-bully convictions went from 498 to 1,286; an increase of 150%.[77]

Helpful resources used to compile this list

www.helpguide.org/mental/cyber-bullying.htm

www.kidpower.org/library/article/cyber-bullying/

www.cyberbullying.us/Top_Ten_Tips_Teens_Prevention.pdf

www.dailymail.co.uk/news/article-2233428/Police-grapple-internet-troll-epidemic-convictions-posting-online-abuse-soar-150-cent-just-years.html#ixzz2gIKCULzy

· · · · ·

Bullying is killing our kids.
Being different is killing our kids
and the kids who are bullying
are dying inside. We have to save our
kids whether they are bullied or they
are bullying. They are all in pain.

CAT CORA

· · · · ·

6 Tips if You are a
Victim of Cyberbullying

(1) Seek assistance from a trusted adult including a parent, a teacher or a counselor.

(2) Do not delete messages from cyberbullies. You do not have to read the messages but keep them as evidence.

(3) Do not reply to the cyberbullies. Your responses serve as encouragement and instill them with a sense of power or influence.

(4) Block the cyberbully.

(5) Report the problem to your Internet service provider, the website and the police.

6 You cannot control the actions of cyberbullies but you can control the way you react. If they get to you, they win.

Helpful resource
kidsafe.com/105/what-to-do-if-you-are-the-victim-of-cyber-bullying

• • • • •

I realized that bullying never has to do with you. It's the bully who's insecure.

SHAY MITCHELL

• • • • •

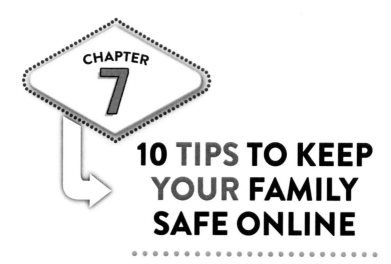

10 TIPS TO KEEP YOUR FAMILY SAFE ONLINE

(1) Do not post pictures of your children wearing nametags.

(2) Do not post vacation departure and return dates.

(3) Keep your Wi-Fi secure and password protected.

(4) Do not post pictures of license plates, addresses or other personal information in the background.

(5) Do not include your full name, address or birth date on your public profiles. Less is always preferable.

(6) Do not post items that reveal your personal daily schedule or habits.

(7) Practice safe browsing and only use secure websites. Look for "https://" when using your credit card. The "s" stands for secure.

(8) Read the online privacy policies VERY carefully. Most sites describe how they use your information.

(9) Insist your children select nicknames when they use online interactive gaming devices including Xbox Live, Nintendo, etc. Use parental controls to protect your children.

(10) Discuss the potential dangers of online use with your children. Keep the lines of communication open.

●　●　●　●　●

"I work in areas related to child protection and family safety, women's empowerment, the creation of opportunities for youth, and culture and tourism. Daunting? Yes. Impossible? No. In fact, such challenges energize me."

QUEEN RANIA OF JORDAN

●　●　●　●　●

BUSINESS AND TEAM RESOURCES

I have written this book in a short, easy to digest format in order to encourage families, teams and organizations to share and discuss these important concepts. Although I have suggested some prompts, feel free to develop any format that suits your needs.

Discussion Prompts for Your Family, Team or Organization

- Describe your digital stamp. How do you want to be remembered?

- Describe a time when you made an offline or online mistake. How did you correct that mistake? What did you learn from that experience?

- Describe a time when you made digital lemonade from digital lemons. Ownership of your mistakes is flawsome!

- Name a statistic in business, your personal life, or this book that made you say "WOW!"

- Assemble into teams and have each team research information on a specific team, company, individual or product. Each team must not only present the top positive item they uncovered and the top negative item they uncovered but also develop an action plan focusing on accentuating those strengths.

- After completing this book, describe one thing you would change about your online presence.

- Break up into teams or pairs and have each team digitally research any individual or organization they hold in high regard. Sketch a digital stamp focusing on esteemed qualities and discuss possible ways to emulate those desired qualities.

EXAMPLE: The American Red Cross is a non-profit organization with the following mission statement:

> *The American Red Cross prevents and alleviates human suffering in the face of emergencies by mobilizing the power of volunteers and the generosity of donors.*[78]

WAYS TO EMULATE: The American Red Cross uses Twitter to promote individual success stories of people doing good. I too can do good and will take five minutes per day to pay it forward and post positive words about people who have nurtured and supported me.

• • • • •

"Individual commitment to a group effort—that is what makes a team work, a company work, a society work, a civilization work."

VINCE LOMBARDI

• • • • •

GENERAL QUIZ

1. **When you make a mistake online or offline, the best course of action is:**

   a. Delete any mention of the mistake and maintain a low profile.

   b. Attempt to hide the mistake and refute all accusations.

   c. "Spin" the story or shift blame.

   d. Immediately and publicly accept responsibility for the mistake and describe the steps you are taking to rectify the mistake.

2. **True or False: To encourage online simplicity, all users of social media sites must have multiple accounts for each site.**

   ❏ True

   ❏ False

3. **What rule should you follow when posting around sensitive topics including religion and politics?**

   a. Keep your argument strictly emotional. Strong emotion demonstrates your passion.

   b. Present factual information and avoid combative dialogue.

   c. Vent your strong disapproval of someone's posting around these topics.

   d. Always write the post in order to convert someone to your way of thinking.

4. **When emotionally upset it is best to:**

   a. Post everything you are thinking as quickly as possible before you lose your strong emotion.

   b. Breathe deeply, count to 10, and then post.

   c. Call a friend and shriek your anger.

   d. Cancel your service provider.

5. **When you see a negative post about yourself or your organization's service, the best approach is:**

   a. Acknowledge the correct statements and apologize for any errors.

   b. Ignore the post.

   c. State that the negative post is incorrect but do not provide details.

   d. Post negative comments about the person who posted the remarks.

6. **When an online series of comments becomes emotionally heated, it is best to:**

   a. Win the argument with sarcastic comments.

   b. Breathe deeply and wait for your emotions to calm down before responding in a professional manner.

   c. Ignore the comments and stop posting any replies.

   d. Post a nasty comment on Twitter.

7. **The art of being "FLAWsome" involves:**

   a. Acknowledging your mistake or flaw while identifying steps to correct that error.

   b. Purchasing expensive dental equipment.

   c. Pointing out your competitors' flaws.

   d. Assuming an arrogant manner especially when you know you made a mistake.

8. **Topics that become heated quickly include:**

   a. Politics

   b. Religion

   c. Sexual Orientation

   d. All of the above

9. **The new rules of reputation are important for:**

   a. Executives

   b. Teenagers

   c. Employees

   d. Politicians

   e. All of the Above

10. **Often what gets people into trouble isn't the actual crime committed, but the:**

    a. Cover-up

    b. Technology

    c. Smoking gun

    d. Money involved

Answers to Quiz:
1. d 2. b 3. b 4. b 5. a 6. b 7. a 8. d 9. e 10. a

QUIZ FOR ATHLETIC TEAMS

1. **If you have a problem with your coach, the best step is:**

    a. Post the issue on Twitter before speaking with your coach.

    b. Talk privately with your coach about the issue.

    c. Tell everyone you know to get his or her advice.

    d. Talk to the press.

2. **True or False: You should constantly update the status of an injury or personal issue on social media.**

    ❑ True

    ❑ False

3. **To help motivate your team and "psych-out" an upcoming opponent you should:**

    a. Post inflammatory comments on social media sites.

    b. Post the wide point spread in favor of your team on Twitter.

    c. Motivate your teammates inside the locker room or during practice.

    d. Post unflattering remarks about specific players on the opposing team.

4. **If you are being hazed or bullied by a teammate, you should:**

    a. Ask that teammate(s) to stop.

    b. Approach the captain of the team and ask for assistance.

    c. Approach and discuss the issue with the coach.

    d. All of the above in this order.

    e. None of the above.

5. **When someone posts negative comments about you personally, it is best to:**

    a. Ignore the post or respond in a calm, focused manner.

    b. Blame others and minimize your involvement.

    c. Find something negative to say about that person.

    d. Post the scenario on Facebook.

6. **When an online series of comments becomes emotionally heated, it is best to:**

    a. Win the argument with unkind or sarcastic remarks.

    b. Breathe deeply, count to 10, and then post responsibly.

    c. Have your boyfriend or girlfriend posting from his or her own account in your defense.

    d. Unfriend that person.

7. **Family, friends, boyfriends or girlfriends must understand:**

   a. Negative posts or comments about the team or an opponent are a direct reflection on you and your team.

   b. Negative posts or comments can result in strained relationships with the press and the coach.

   c. Pointing out the flaws of your competitors is completely unacceptable.

   d. All of the above.

8. **Game plans should be:**

   a. Kept to yourself.

   b. Shared with friends and family.

   c. Posted to social media so you can attract more followers.

   d. Disclosed to friendly press member who travel with the team.

9. **Participation on social media during the season is:**

   a. A necessity

   b. A privilege

   c. Best used during the game

10. **Often what gets people into trouble isn't actually the crime committed, but the:**

    a.   Money involved

    b.   Cover-up

    c.   Technology

    d.   Smoking gun

11. **The best way to increase my value with pro scouts via social media is:**

    a.   Post three to five times per day.

    b.   Post the reasons you would make a great pro.

    c.   Use social media to compare and contrast your athletic abilities with current professional athletes.

    d.   Be genuine, interact with fans in a professional manner and work hard.

    e.   Interact and "friend" professional agents via social media.

12. **When is it appropriate to use profane language or racial slurs in a joking manner?**

    a.   With teammates because this type of banter bonds the team.

    b.   With select friends who understand the context and your sense of humor.

    c.   With the opposite sex.

    d.   Never.

13. **The best way to increase popularity and gain followers on Twitter is:**

   a. Show a genuine interest in others and try to provide them value.

   b. Do something controversial.

   c. Post frequently about anything that crosses your mind.

   d. Tweet comments about your teammates or coaches.

14. **If you are not getting sufficient playing time, you should:**

   a. Lobby for more playing time via social media.

   b. Convince several close friends to post your displeasure on social media.

   c. Discuss your concerns with the coaches in a private conversation.

   d. Become friends with the press and describe your displeasure in great detail so they can write an article.

15. **If an attractive male or female flirts with you online, you should:**

   a. Use social media to develop the relationship before meeting in person.

   b. Send impressive information about yourself.

   c. Meet in person after you check their digital profile.

   d. Take a snapshot and forward to your best friend.

16. **If you find reading comments about yourself on social media is negatively affecting your athletic performance or hurting your class work, you should:**

   a. Take a break from social media until the season or semester is over.

   b. Pay external social media agencies or consultants to manage your accounts.

   c. Hire a sports agent to help you manage your life.

   d. Watch videos on TMZ.

   ### Answers to Quiz:

   1. b   2. b (false)   3. c   4. d   5. a   6. b   7. d   8. a
   9. b   10. b   11. d   12. d   13. a   14. c   15. c   16. a

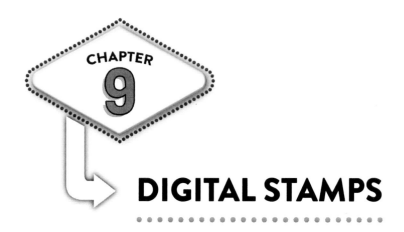

DIGITAL STAMPS

A Digital Stamp is a permanent collection and culmination of your digital footprints and digital shadows. Your digital stamp matters 5 seconds from now, 5 years from now, 50 years from now, and 500 years from now.

I asked individuals and companies to submit the digital STAMP they want to leave on this world. Here are some responses. You submit your own at *equalman@equalman.com*. We will absolutely add more to the next edition. If your stamp didn't make this edition, it can certainly be in the next edition. Heartfelt thanks to my loyal supporters; this book would not exist without you! As for me, my desired STAMP is:

"Be a Digital Dale Carnegie by motivating others to their best life, leadership & legacy. Honor my family & God."
@equalman

"Exploring possibilities, putting useful apps to work every day, and contributing to the body of digital knowledge."
Margie Putnam

"Successful social media butterfly with high profile within music, marketing and radio circles. Starting in radio working with unsigned bands, she has worked her way up through marketing, music journalism and social media to become one of the most hardworking, trustworthy and friendly people to work with. With a passion for all things social and creative, she puts effort into everything she does to make sure she can help others achieve their goals."

Cheryl Hughes, UK
cheryl.hughes@drllimited.co.uk

"My legacy, he loved Jesus, loved his family, great family man & wonderful businessman. In that order."

Greg Baily @bigtimemarketer

"The web is my playground."

@kwerner

"That I made life fun."

@phylliskhare

"To have made a difference to people I touch."

@thelinkedinman

"Help Higher Education Sector understand how social media can improve customer service/relationship management."

@davidgirlinguk

"I want every one of my academic papers and studies and lectures to be accessible and available to all (+free)."

@JohnGirdwood

"She was real. She cared. She connected!"

@SCMSJanine

"I want my legacy to be a rich narrative of connections, experience and expertise."

@TSCollier217

"Compassionate connector, insatiably curious, convinced sleep is overrated."

@ScratchMM

"10 years from now I would like people to see how geeky I was in 2013."

@JeanRicher

"I would like my digital legacy to be an understanding of how digital is part of everything but is nothing on its own."

@SimonSalento

"Always cared about others well being and made it a point to put others in front of himself."

@joshharcus

"Impacted how teachers & parents embrace educating children on building relationships & protecting their personal brands using social media."

Scott Wild

"We listened because he did."

@arnoldtijerina7

"She didn't "talk at," she "listened to" and engaged with her audience on a more personable level."

@PamSahota

"Life is full of seasons, but at the end of mine, I want others to find that I spoke for those who couldn't speak for themselves."

@JanieSikes

"Be Real. Live your passion. Stay present. Never let your mind second guess your heart."

@springboardw

"I impacted other lives in a positive way. I was passionate about life and lived with a true sense of gratitude. I created my own path."

Jason DeAmato

"Andrew was a great father and manager. His specialty was growing online businesses in good and bad economic times. He made everyone laugh."

Andrew Artemenko

"Develop my business and career. It's my digital CV..."

@paulpingles

"Create awareness for, visibility of & support to people in need who are less fortunate than us!"

@jonrpeters

"He challenged the established norms in the realm of digital marketing to facilitate growth of companies he is associated with."

Arun Varma

"Helping broaden narrow minds."

@earthianne

"He believed in the ability of mankind to change the World."

Jean Baptiste

"He loved and invested in a younger generation, encouraging them to be remarkable for the glory of God."

@alvinreid

"I'm the tweep behind 'The Greatest Customer Service Story Ever Told.'"

@JillianMktng

"He inspired and entertained, he blessed many, he was a success as a man."

Ryan Bethea

"He was a relational architect who helped Higher Education embrace social media as a new "normal" while wearing sweatervests."

John Hill

"He invested his life into mine, taught me to live wide awake and step into the fullest and best version of myself."

Scott Schimmel

"Strived to promote genuine values in work, family, friendship, love and everyday life."

Jason Rubley "Rubes"

"I follow the creator, servant, CrossFiter, firefighter, helper, Student, Tennessean, technology enthusiasts, leader."

@C_RSmith

"Inspired others to live a great story through healthy living, love of family, community service and a sense of adventure."

Shanna Kurpe

"He was great in virtue."

Maciejobza

"I hope to they see how to alter their children's legacy by learning how to leave the planet better than they found it."

Kristina Summers

"Like Kipling, I know something of the things which are underneath, and of the things which are beyond the frontier."

Jim Nico

"Christoph showed that communication is happiness and the essential thing in life."
Christoph Jeschke

"Layne continues to spread her love of humanity through her works and writings. She lives happily with her wife of 110 years and their dog."
Layne Holley

"I overcame the pain of losing an infant and was a loved and loving father and husband. And, I gave my boys the gift of writing. Beautifully."
Mark Irvine

"Known for artistic expression, Laurie developed & nurtured relationships & influenced action & change by listening & sharing relevant & compelling information."
Laurie Wakefield

"We will transform collaboration in Brazil through the power of education, technology and fun!"
Luiz Irumé & Sâmara Irumé, E-continuus Inc.

"A freedom fighter who believed everyone is a leader. She encouraged others to stand up, do something, be meaningful."
Nancy Beth Guptill

"She proved that kindness and caring is the true key to success."
Katelyn Auclair

"She brought genetic carrier status out of the closet."
Jane Belland Karwoski, MyBlueGenome

"A freedom fighter who believed everyone is a leader. She encouraged others to stand up, do something, be meaningful."
@SweetMarketing

"She made all the little things count, no matter how small, happy is happy."

@sarahJAYYallday

"A really good teacher."

Megan Peters

"Enabling footprints to broaden the reach & access in closing the digital & social divide."

@mwthomasSCRM

"She inspired and empowered generations of authors."

@LisaTener

"He turned an obsession with Social Media into a series of successful businesses, and he had a BLAST every step of the way."

Michael McClure

"A leader who inspired others to create opportunities and act based on their passion in life."

@akassab

"That I helped out people who were in need and all the different organizations I was involved in and all the good I had done around the world."

Cole Menzel

"That I became a successful Music Supervisor, I'd want my life to be reflected as a good one. Someone who achieved what they wanted."

Erin Zins (@erinzins)

"I'd want my digital legacy to sum up my life. It would be really interesting to just look back at anyone, and see what their lives like."

Brandon Wilton

"For helping people in some way, like giving up something important to me or giving my life for someone to live or prosper better."

Jason Ratcliff

"I would want it to talk about the things that I accomplished, my family, the people who were close to me."

Boochi Kashinkunti

"That I loved my family more than they will ever know and I was pretty good at writing IEP's."

Vicki Peterman

"1. I did not do something just because everyone else did. 2. When I am tagged in photos, I look like a swamp monster. 3. I dressed FABULOUSLY."

Abby Lawley

"The hard work I put into becoming the person I am today and that it allows me and my friends to look back and be proud of who we were."

Brock Kamrath

"An article about me graduating from Mizzou, my work in the field of nuclear power, and solve the energy crisis that we will continue to face."

Jessie Jennings

"To show that I am a kind and selfless person, that I rather think of others than myself. All in all for have a big heart."

Meghan McMurray

"That I made a difference in peoples' lives. That I did all I could to help others who couldn't help themselves and I succeeded."

Tricia Morgan

"My digital legacy stamp would simply be "Grace Gollon is awesome.""

Grace Gollon

"A website with a short bio about me, and how I started a nationally-known organization."

Leah Mergen @missLMergen

"A woman who loved God, her family, was blessed beyond her wildest dreams and was a blessing to others."

Julie Zara

"Tyler was loyal to his friends and family. He loved where he came from (Riverton IL). He was patriotic, happy and thankful for living in the USA!"

Tyler Curry @Tyler_Curry89

"She's a leader that's purposeful, positive and present and because of that she was able to empower thousands of women to live their dream."

Julie Timm

"A strong woman who survived many tests in her lifetime. She beat breast cancer and selflessly participated in research for The Cure. She gave all that she had to her family & friends. She loved unconditionally and was loved endlessly."

Mary Tolley

As a microlending nonprofit, PeopleFund would like to be remembered as being a "hand up, not hand out."

Miku Sakamoto

"She was a caring individual who used her creative gifts and talents to help others!"

Jennifer Frey

"She inspired people to think big and achieve things they never thought possible. She revolutionized education."

Courtney O'Connell (@CourtOconnell)

"Glass half-full kind of girl. I want her on my team. Always growing and learning. She helped me (fill in the blank). Let's shake it up."

Katie Beals (@katiebeals)

"Absolutely nothing. The world is the playground of the living. I hope they enjoy it as much as I did."

John Cimmino

"Passionate, Nerdy, Student Affairs Professional, Loves public speaking and helping students at every turn. D&D, MMOs, books, Whedonite."

Michael Ambyth

"Cynthia engages people in social justice through media, technology and artistic expression in Higher Ed & Student Affairs communities."

Cynthia Kaselis (@CynthiaKaselis)

"My ABCs: Always be part of something greater than yourself. Bring out the best in others. Create & conquer. #Rutgers #JerseyStrong #highered"

Sandra Golis (@SandraG1117)

"I am a Student Affairs professional, world traveler and avid knitter. I want to make the world a better place one stitch at a time."

Kolrick Greathouse (@KolGreat)

"Hard work pays off and a little faith goes a long way. I've loved,lost, and made mistakes but I LIVED! I love people. Jersey Strong-Go RU!"

Amber McNeil (@LeonaSp10)

"That I've made the world a little bit happier through my efforts. Happiness through fulfillment, laughter and connections."

Dustin Ramsdell (@highered_geek)

"Dedicated father and college professional that solved the problems of the world through authentic helpfulness, one college student at a time."

Bobby Bullard (@BBullard7)

"Tim helps churches grow through communicating better."

Tim Peters (@timrpeters)

"I want individuals to change the way they think about finance and economics and apply practical finance tips to their lives."

Sagar Lakhani (@sman9000)

"Someone who harnessed the power of online professionally and personally, embraced the digital evolution and rolled with its daily changes."

Peter Hughes (@hughespjh)

"I'd like to be remembered as a true professional, objective, dedicated to my craft, who treated people well and added value to their lives."

Steve Amoia (@worldfootballcm)

"God, country & family. Happy 2 know @equalman—a great thought leader & person. Love to Mary-Beth, Lucia, Eva & Mica, & my brother Glenn!"

Stephen Selby (@StephenFSelby)

"Number crunching photographer who loves riding my bicycle really, really fast. I live with MS and write about it on The Lesion Journals."
Christie Germans (@lesionjournals)

"I hope people find a legacy. Family members can look back and know exactly who I was. That the internet showcases a snapshot of life today."
Lisa Simonson (@PRladyLisa)

"I don't define myself solely by what I do or what I have achieved. I love my life and I love what I do. Each day more of what I do reflects what I love to do."
Melissa Silva (@ChiaMelly)

"I tried to help people in every way I could. I spread the truth and loved my family."
Jason Bhatti (@bhattibytes)

"Follower of Jesus. Love of my wife, kids, family & friends. Big time business leader, marketer & innovator. Global education philanthropist."
Greg Bailey (@bigtimemarketer)

"A digital native who loves connecting with people. Always learning new stuff and likes helping internet startups & businesses."
Neeraj Thakur (@NeerajT4)

"As a Nara-born editor who created useful English learning materials for Japanese and also as a tour guide for foreigners coming to Japan."
Yusuke Takeuchi (@sosorasora)

"Evidence of his work expanding the understanding between technology and education all while making sure students were achieving their goals."

Josh Kohnert (@JoshKohnert)

"Next generation leader that equips & empowers leaders to leverage today's tools, trends & talent to thrive tomorrow."

Ryan Jenkins (@theRyanJenks)

"True nobility is not about being better than anyone else; it's about being better than you used to be."

Rod Ponce (@rodponce)

"Connector, Empathy driven, Humane."

Vikram Mekala (@mekalav)

"Rolled with the #Apple Crew while still being able to hang with the #Google Gang, Digital Ninja, Author of @ichurchmethod"

Jason Caston (@jasoncaston)

"I'd like people (or robots) in 2113 to find a connected, curious, compassionate Molly who eventually learned to express herself in 140 chara (intentionally cut off)."

Molly Rucki (@mollyrucki)

"Social & Digital Marketing Strategist, Marketing Data Scientist, Competitive Runner, Assistant Professor, University of Missouri–St. Louis"

Perry D. Drake (@pddrake)

"I tried to help people in every way I could. I spread the truth and loved my family."

Jason Bhatti (@bhattibytes)

"To be a motivator and connector of small business owners increasing their revenues while supporting God's work."
Mike Saunders (@marketinghuddle)

"A true community developer – at home, in my neighbourhood, at work, online. One coffee mug at a time."
Lindsey Fair (@lindseyfair)

"@tamcdonald, aka Tim McDonald: Builder of communities, not networks. Teacher via being a perpetual student. Be happy. Do good. #ArtOfWork"
Tim McDonald (@tamcdonald)

"Won't be satisfied until we actually change something about the world, make it better."
Brian Reich (@brianreich)

"Jordan loved life, and cared passionately about humanity. He was loved by many for enabling them to follow their dreams."
Jordan Skoe (@JordanSkole)

"Dr. Syb truly lived, loved & learned. Her legacy of passion, engagement & wisdom remains contagious. Catch & share it."
Sybril Bennett (@drsyb)

"Family matters most. Lots of love to our family Helga, Karl, Óli, Sibbi, Grímur, Kalli and their families. Gummi and family."
Gudmundur Karl Karlsson (@gummikalli)

"Author of the #1 selling LinkedIn book The Power Formula for LinkedIn Success, LinkedIn Trainer, Speaker, Consultant, CPA...love cat."
Wayne Breitbarth (@waynebreitbarth)

"I hope folks would discover I'm a teacher, philanthropist, recognized speaker, business builder and great dad and husband."
Mike Merrill (@MikeDMerrill)

"Business thinker who tries to democratize access to opportunity."

Dorie Clark (@dorieclark)

"Dependable, Honest, Respectful, Trustworthy, Kind, Generous, Intelligent. Mother, Wife, Sister, Daughter. Passion for life, music, art, peace."

April McCormack (@ivycoils)

"Paul was a really nice guy who made a difference in the lives of the individuals that he met."

Paul Goldenberg (@bluefrogpaul)

"Always present, prepared and passionate about work, friends and family."

Nancy Kohutek

"President and Co-Founder of pidalia & racut – Mad Man, Speaker, Technologist, and Sushi Connoisseur."

Scott Dubois (@ScottDubois)

"Builder of marketing ideas that irrevocably connect people and brands."

Chris Perkins (@TopherPerkins)

"I hope that I've made a positive impact on people helping find their passions in life, and had some fun along the way."

Dustin Ramsdell (@highered_geek)

"I hope that, 100 years from now, my online legacy will provide an accurate and consistent picture of who I was – both online and IRL."

Tyrone Hooge (@tyronehooge)

"Proud father of Sara, Sindri and Sunna. Solution designer focused on optimizing businesses with innovative technology. Loves a challenge."
Ingólfurorsteinsson (@IngolfurTh)

"They were honest and fair and raised a good family."
Philip Kiger

"Chandler Vreeland"
Chandler Vreeland

"Aproveite a vida! =)"
Leonardo Magalhaes

"Christie is a number crunching photographer who loves riding her bicycle really, really fast and lives with Multiple Sclerosis (MS)."
Christie Germans (@lesionjournals)

"I found my passion late in life—teaching. So I hope my digital stamp will show that I helped my students find their passion and encouraged them to reach their full potential."
Dale Blasingame (@daleblasingame)

"A leader who inspired others to create opportunities and act based on their passion in life."
Alex Kassab (@akassab)

"Hopefully not too much cat content I posted ;)"
David Redelberger (@davidfromkassel)

"Proud Mother of Darcy and Shea who made the world a better place by just being themselves."
Nikki Moran

"Someone who started 3D character animation in Mauritius; someone who started the first 3D Animation Training in Mauritius; an entrepreneur who always tried new things, and was never scared of the uncertainties of life."

Satyen Bhujun

"Create a better world by working quietly behind the scenes to connect people, spark ideas & catalyze change under the guise of serendipity."

Jennifer Barrett (@jenbarrett)

"IF OPPORTUNITY DOESN'T KNOCK, BUILD A DOOR."

Piers Brown (@bohonews)

"I love web development, social media, cats and music. I like my online world to cover all of those things."

Jess Wearn (@helloitsjess)

"Many moments of laughter, leadership and love."

Lizzie Williams (@LLLizzie)

"I would hope that people find that I created more than consumed, helped more than hindered, loved, took risks, made mistakes and learned."

Dave Banas (@davebanas)

"@arnobiomorelix, social entrepreneur from PESSOA Institute, an organization teaching entrepreneurship to remote communities in South America"

Arnobio Morelix (@arnobiomorelix)

"I hope people will find that I found my passion, loved my job, worked hard & made a difference in higher education & a student's experience."

Cortney Brewer (@Cortbrew)

"A great husband, dad and leader who loves family, the auto industry and science, technology, engineering & math education."

Mark Johnson

"Connector of remarkable strategies, ideas, business and people...Passionate about family, an active lifestyle and giving back."

Patrick Sitkins (@patricksitkins)

"I would like people to find photos of my family, friends and beloved dog Bentley. I believe pictures and videos speak louder than words."

Stephanie Corritori (@scorritoricbsi)

• • • • •

*The supreme quality for leadership
is unquestionably integrity. Without it,
no real success is possible, no matter
whether it is on a section gang,
a football field, in an army,
or in an office.*

DWIGHT D. EISENHOWER

• • • • •

The following submissions from current high school teachers offer advice to their students

"Keep in mind that all you do on the Internet leaves a footprint, a digital footprint."

Lowell, MA High School Teacher

"People will judge you by what you post; how do you want to be known?"

Audrey Ennamorati, High School Teacher

"Protect your privacy. The whole world does not need to know everything about you."

Love, Mom & High School Teacher

"Don't put anything out there you wouldn't want your Nana to read."

High School Teacher and Nana

"Don't post anything that 15 years from now would prevent you from getting a government job."

Joan, High School Teacher

"Know that what you put online stays online. You can just as easily use technology to learn about the world as you can to waste time. You have the power to make a positive change in the world, so use it well."

Kelly Neely, High School Teacher

"Big brother is watching and now he is sharing."

High School Teacher

"Nothing is ever erased off the Internet."

Leisha O'Brien, High School Teacher

1. Once it is on the Internet, it is there to stay.
   There is no delete
2. Don not hide behind anonymity. That's another form
   of bullying.
3. With great power comes great responsibility."

Bryce Mattie

"Never post a picture you wouldn't want a prospective employer to see."

Jakki Therrien

"I still the Use the old adage 'if you don't have anything nice to say, don't say anything at all.' It still works for posting on Facebook!"

Krista Hoey

"A pic on Facebook or any other site is worth a 1,000 words. Make sure those words impact you and those around you in a positive way."

Sean Wasson

"Don't post anything you would be ashamed to tell your grandma."

tristan.noyes@ef.com

"Use privacy settings."

Richard Barnaby

"Just like in real life, watch out for creepy vans with no windows...aka: watch out for people you don't know."

**Ms. Caitlin Engle, Science Department,
Norwalk High School**

"If you do want to see it on a billboard...don't post it online."

Anita Lotti

• • • • •

"The foundation stones for a balanced success are honesty, character, integrity, faith, love and loyalty."

ZIG ZIGLAR

• • • • •

"Remember nothing is ever really deleted."
Kellie Freitas

"Don't put anything online that you wouldn't want printed in the front page of your local newspaper."
Richard Marrese

"Find balance between the digital world and the analog world."
David Peling

"I'd recommend that students not be afraid of using technology and that they use it to practice their spelling and grammar."
Rick Lavoie

"If you wouldn't say it in person, don't say it online!"
Emily LeBlanc-Perrone

"Be aware that your future employers, friends, family and self will see what you put online. It never disappears."
Marisa Haralson

"Keep it classy."
Tara Roberts

"Digital can't be easily destroyed like a note you passed to your friend."

Kim Vigil

"Loving father that enjoys traveling w/family, cooking to music, a great story, and a hearty laugh over a cold beer."

@VictorGaxiola

SUCCESS INSIGHTS FROM INDIVIDUALS

Please find below four stories that will inspire you to achieve your best. These are personal insights from individuals that have achieved success in this digital age. They faced a challenge head on and came out stronger as a result of it. Hopefully their personal stories will help you the next time you are faced with a difficult decision or challenge. They have been kind enough to include their contact information so feel free to follow them or connect with them.

Marc Colando:
Taking the moral high road pays off

I remember one particular story from the go-go Web 1.0 days of the late-90's. My agency in Atlanta was growing at a fantastic clip, and attracting lots of great employees and clients. There's more info at http://ipi.net for the curious.

One day, a client asked us to bid on a project from a newly formed business unit. The task? Build an online system that would prioritize patients in the emergency room based on their credit score. Ewww. We respectfully passed, citing a philosophical conflict. A few days later, we got a call from the lead client, who would go on to be a high-ranking global executive. "You know, one of your competitors will make a million dollars from this project if you don't." He's right. They probably did.

This test to my 25-year old self was the first of many that would determine how well I'd be able to sleep at night. Since then, I almost certainly haven't always done the "right" thing. And I've definitely left millions on the table for every million I've made. But, if you connect with me on LinkedIn, you'll see a recommendation that remains my proudest business accomplishment. A former client writes that besides having my share of talent and skills, I am a "[good] human being." I use this comment as a standard measure in my life now. Am I doing my best to be a good person today?

Follow me on Twitter (@mcolando), hit me up on Facebook or find me on LinkedIn to let me know how I'm doing. I love new ideas and I'd be excited to follow your own stories of inspiration as they unfold.

Marc Colando, @mcolando

• • • • •

"How could you have a soccer team if all were goalkeepers? How would it be an orchestra if all were French horns?"

DESMOND TUTU

• • • • •

Lisa Tener:
If you don't like something, change it

After it took Lisa Tener seven years to go from idea to holding a published book in her hands, she decided it shouldn't take that long! She began helping aspiring self-help authors write quality books and book proposals quickly. It worked. Many of her clients write a first draft or proposal in 8-12 weeks and then sign book deals.

"I'm invested in helping people write stand-out books that make a big difference in readers' lives, get published by top publishers or are self published and win awards. With social media, I found I can't spread myself thin. I needed to prioritize, so I focused on blogging which:

- Helps people find you on Google, since Google rewards excellent extensive content

- Can lead to blogging for a national platform: For many of my clients that means Psychology Today or the Huffington Post—which helped several clients obtain book deals.

- Lets me share client successes, helping them sell books and providing practical advice to readers.

- Cultivates relationships with your readers—in my case, many readers gain confidence to invest in high end programs knowing I can help them write the quality book they want: Rather than having to sell my services on a phone call, people know they want to work with me before calling.

LESSON LEARNED: Focus social media in areas that build engagement and support your highest priority goals. Play to your strengths and interests; for me, that's writing."

Visit Lisa's blogs at lisatener.com, how-to-write-a-book.com and the Huffington Post.

Lisa Tener — LisaTener.com, @LisaTener

Kamron Karington:
Silly String can be your savior

Handcuffed and pacing a Hollywood jail cell, Kamron Karington was grinning. Thirty minutes earlier a cloud of Silly String, aimed at a friend's car, landed instead on the windshield of a passing LAPD patrol car. The officer was not amused. But the opportunity of a lifetime was at hand for Karrington.

The next day "Manager of Cause And Effect Arrested For Felony Silly-String Assault on a Police Officer" was a national story (http://bit.ly/silly-string). A much-needed jolt of publicity instantly catapulted a struggling band onto the *Billboard* chart, a national MTV tour and a quarter million records sold. A freak occurrence involving Silly String was leveraged into a magic carpet ride.

Today, Karington's company, Repeat Returns harnesses social media to build client's sales and rocket national brands up the Nielsen charts. Karington says, "by making digital personal, meaningful and fun, we can drive a word-of-mouth buying frenzy at the push of a button, but more importantly, identify and nurture brand champions who promote and protect on behalf of brands they love."

LESSON LEARNED: "A freak occurrence can take you up, or take you down. Fast. And bad news, raging customers or disgruntled employees can poison your reputation while you sleep. Going public with my silly-string arrest was my decision. Today, it's anyone's. Defenders and destroyers alike are prowling the social landscape. You must communicate the good, and get ahead of the bad before it blows up in your face. If your defenders don't craft your reputation, your detractors will."

Kamron Karington

Arnobio Morelix:
Making success an option for everyone

In a hundred years, the notion that businesses can pursue profits alone at the expense of society will probably be outdated. And it might sound as archaic as the early 1900s' use of child labor sounds to us today.

This trend is fueled by increasing transparency in the business world. As companies come under public scrutiny, practices that were common—such as disregard for the environment or sweatshop-like working conditions for whole communities—are not acceptable anymore.

In Brazil, however, there was a group that was invisible to society. Remote communities and indigenous tribes, in areas including the Amazon jungle and the arid backcountry, usually got the short end of economic development. To help solve this problem, social entrepreneur Arnobio Morelix co-founded the PESSOA Institute. PESSOA teaches people in these communities how to start their own businesses, including participating in the online economy. The project has trained more than 2,000 people for free since its inception in 2009.

For his project, Arnobio has recently been nominated for the Inspiring Young Innovators of Brazil prize, organized by Revista Veja, the largest circulation magazine in the country. In addition, in order to expand the mission globally, Arnobio is now working on the pre-launch phase for Origem Lab, a not-for-profit accelerator that will host entrepreneurs from around the world at Google Fiberhood, the startup community served by Google Fiber's ultra-speed internet.

What happens on Vegas definitely stays on YouTube. Arnobio is working so that what happens in the Amazon jungle also does.

Arnobio Morelix (@arnobiomorelix)

GLOSSARY

CATFISH: Someone who uses social media and other digital tools to create a false persona. Typically used to attract online romances. For example, the user posts a beautiful picture and an impressive biography under a false name.

Former Notre Dame Linebacker and NFL player Manti Te'o indicated he was a victim of catfishing.

"Catfish" is a 2010 movie that tells the story of a young man who develops an online relationship with a woman who is vastly different from her Facebook profile.

The origin of the term could stem from the movie or the restaurant practice of substituting a cheaper fish in place of customer's more expensive selection.

CYBERBULLY: To tease, insult or make fun of another person online. The intent is to destroy the target's reputation. Cyberbullying is often considered a criminal offense. Offline bullying laws apply to online behavior.

DIGTIAL FOOTPRINT: Everything you post about yourself online. Examples include status update, blog post, photo/video upload, text, tweet, etc.

DIGITAL LEGACY: (Synonym of Digital Stamp) A permanent collection and culmination of your digital footprints and digital shadows. Your digital stamp matters 5 seconds from now, 5 years from now, 50 years from now and 500 years from now. This term generally applies to your digital stamp after the death of a person or an organization

DIGITAL SHADOWS: The items other people post about you. This includes your online and offline actions. Almost every person and organization has a digital shadow, even if he or she does not use online tools.

DIGITAL STAMP: A permanent collection and culmination of your digital footprints and digital shadows. Your digital stamp matters 5 seconds from now, 5 years from now, 50 years from now and 500 years from now.

FLAWSOME: Something or someone who is fantastic yet flawed. This can be a person, company, product, organization or object. Flawsome combines the words Flaws and Awesome. As a company or individual, you can prove how awesome you are when you make a mistake and take actions to correct that mistake.

Non-business example: Chicago's Wrigley Field is old with small uncomfortable seats, insufficient parking and overly expensive drinks, yet it is a totally Flawsome ballpark.

POST-IT FORWARD: Similar to the offline act of paying it forward in which an individual performs an act of kindness without expecting something in return such as paying for a stranger's expired parking meter. Online examples include endorsing someone on LinkedIn, positively posting about someone else's success on Twitter or Facebook, liking someone's post, re-tweeting, etc.

RETWEET: A retweet is a re-posting of someone else's tweet. Twitter's retweet feature helps you and others quickly share that tweet with all your followers. Sometimes people type RT at the beginning of a tweet to indicate they are re-posting someone else's content. This is not an official Twitter command or feature but signifies the person is quoting another user's Tweet. It is analogous to forwarding an email.

TROLL: Online user who posts inflammatory posts on message boards, blogs, comment section or product reviews in order to incite controversy and argument. Their arguments and comments are often off-topic.

Wikipedia definition: In Internet slang, a troll (/ tro l/, / tr l/) is a person who sows discord on the Internet by starting arguments or upsetting people, by posting inflammatory, extraneous or off-topic messages in an online community (such as a forum, chat room or blog), either accidentally or with the deliberate intent of provoking readers into an emotional response or of otherwise disrupting normal on-topic discussion.

TWEETING: The act of posting digital messages in a 140 character or less format on the popular micro-blogging platform Twitter.

• • • • •

"Integrity does not come in degrees—low, medium or high. You either have integrity or you do not."

TONY DUNGY

• • • • •

NOTES

1 Leslie Meredith, "Internet Safety for Kids: Almost All Children Under 2 Have A Digital Footprint," *Huffington Post via AVG Study,* January 10, 2013, www.huffingtonpost.com/2013/01/10/children-internet-safety_n_ 2449721.html

2 "Tweeter's Remorse? Some Users Regreat What They've Shared on Social Media," *CBSNewYork,* July 29, 2013, newyork.cbslocal.com/2013/07/29/ tweeters-remorse-some-users-regret-what-theyve-shared-on-social-media/

3 Cecilia Kang, "70 percent of hiring managers say they reject job applicants because of info they find online," *Washington Post,* January 28, 2010, voices.washingtonpost.com/posttech/2010/01/hiring_manager_70_ percent_say.html

4 Zanub Saeed, "McDonald's Menu: Secret Ingredients of Big Mac Secret Sauce Revealed (Video)," *Franchise Herald,* July 15, 2012, www.franchise- herald.com/articles/1801/20120715/mcdonalds-menu-secret-ingredients -big-magic-sauce.htm

5 John Greathouse, "Eight Startup Tips From Mark Zuckerberg," *INFOCHACHKIE,* January 23, 2012, infochachkie.com/8-startup-tips- mark-zuckerberg/

6 Josh Waitzkin, "The Multitasking Virus and the End of Learning? Part 1," *The Blog of Tim Ferris,* www.fourhourworkweek.com/blog/2008/05/25/the-multitasking-virus- 7and-the-end-of-learning-part-1/

7 Reppler Survey, September 27, 2011, blog.reppler.com/2011/09/27/ managing-your-online-image-across-social-netw /

8 www.morganbrown.com/docs/Social%20Networking%20Article%20 (final).pdf

9 Susan Adams, "LinkedIn Got Me Two Great Jobs," *Forbes,* January 19, 2012, www.forbes.com/sites/susanadams/2012/01/19/true-story- linkedin-got-me-two-great-jobs/

10 Deepanjali Pandey, *LinkedIn Press Center,* http://press.linkedin.com/ success-stories

[11] I first heard this word from Marketing Professor's Anne Hadley — check out her great work!

[12] Jennifer Larsen, Maritz Research and Evolve24- Twitter Study. Rep. Maritz Research and Evolve24, September 2011, www.maritzresearch.com/~/media/Files/MaritzResearch/e24/ExecutiveSummaryTwitterPoll.ashx

[13] Laurie Segall, "Boozy Red Cross tweet turns into marketing bonanza for Dogfish Brewery," CNN Money, February, 17, 2011, money.cnn.com/2011/02/17/smallbusiness/dogfish_redcross/index.htm

[14] Jennifer Valentino-Devries, "Hackers Leak IDs Tied to Apple Devices," The Wall Street Journal, September 5, 2012, online.wsj.com/article/SB10000872396390444301704577631721370098002.html?mod=google-news_wsj

[15] Michael Pearson, "The Petraeus affair: A lot more than sex," CNN, November 14, 2012, www.cnn.com/2012/11/12/us/petraeus-cia-resignation

[16] David Kirkpatrick, "The Facebook Effect," Simon & Schuster, February 1, 2011

[17] Sarah Kessler, "Chrysler's Twitter Account Accidentally Drops the F-Bomb," Mashable, March 9, 2011, http://mashable.com/2011/03/09/chrysler-drops-the-f-bomb-on-twitter/

[18] www.acomplaintfreeworld.org/

[19] Shawn Achor, "The happy secret to better work," TEDx Video, May 2011, www.ted.com/talks/shawn_achor_the_happy_secret_to_better_work.html

[20] Candidate Tracking Statistics. Rep. IMPACT Group, April 2010, www.impactgrouphr.com/Libraries/Reports_Trends/Candidate_Tracking_Statistics_April_2010.sflb.ashx

[21] Lindsey Seavert, "Teen creates viral campaign to stop cyberbullies," USA Today, August 17, 2012, usatoday30.usatoday.com/news/health/wellness/story/2012-08-17/teen-twitter-cyberbullies/57120166/1

[22] Brian Bennett, "Ohio State now faces 'failure to monitor'," ESPN, November 11, 2011, http://espn.go.com/college-football/story/_/id/7217079/ncaa-slaps-ohio-state-buckeyes-failure-monitor-charge

[23] Salvador Rodriguez, "Nokia apologizes for faking shots in Lumia 920 camera phone ad," Los Angeles Times, September 7, 2012, articles.latimes.com/2012/sep/07/business/la-fi-nokia-fake-20120907

[24] www.foxnews.com/politics/2011/06/01/rep-weiner-knocks-questions-lewd-photo-says-wont-distracted/#ixzz2Gqz05y4W

[25] John Medina, Brain Rules | Sydni Craig-Hart, "Startling Statistics on the Negative Effects of Multitasking" Profitable Spa. Profitable Spa, n.d.,

[26] John Naish, "Is Multi-tasking Bad for Your Brain? Experts Reveal the Hidden Perils of Juggling Too Many Jobs." Mail Online. Associated Newspapers Ltd, August 11, 2009, www.dailymail.co.uk/health/article-1205669/Is-multi-tasking-bad-brain-Experts-reveal-hidden-perils-juggling-jobs.html#ixzz2mWznauHG

[27] "Multitasking: Switching costs," *American Psychological Association*, www.apa.org/research/action/multitask.aspx

[28] "Many Pedestrians Hit By Cars Are Distracted by Mobile Devices," *Health*, October 2, 2012, http://news.health.com/2012/10/02/many-pedestrians-hit-by-cars-are-distracted-by-mobile-devices/

[29] Josh Waitzkin, "The Multitasking Virus and the End of Learning? Part 1," *The Blog of Tim Ferris*, www.fourhourworkweek.com/blog/2008/05/25/the-multitasking-virus-and-the-end-of-learning-part-1/]

[30] "Microsoft's Bing Caught Copying Google Search Results," *Fox News*, February 1, 2011, www.foxnews.com/tech/2011/02/01/microsofts-bing-caught-copying-google-search-results/

[31] "7 times social networking saved lives," *Mother Nature Network*, November 1, 2010, http://www.mnn.com/green-tech/computers/photos/7-times-social-networking-saved-lives/facebook-rare-donor-found-for-leuk

[32] Research from Albert Mehrabian (UCLA Professor), en.wikipedia.org/wiki/Albert_Mehrabian#Misinterpretation

[33] Carol Kinsey Goman, "10 Simple and Powerful Body Language Tips for 2012," *Forbes*, January 3, 2012, via a study on handshakes by the Income Center for Trade Shows, http://www.forbes.com/sites/carolkinseygoman/2012/01/03/10-simple-and-powerful-body-language-tips-for-2012/

[34] Joseph Grenny, "Antisocial Networks? Hostility on social media rising for 78 percent of users." *Press Room*. Vital Smarts, 10 April, 2013, www.vitalsmarts.com/press/2013/04/antisocial-networks-hostility-on-social-media-rising-for-78-percent-of-users/

[35] Dennis Yang, "Tone Misinterpreted In Half Of All Emails ," *TechDirt*, Feb 13, 2006, http://www.techdirt.com/articles/20060213/1558206.shtml

[36] www.techeblog.com/index.php/tech-gadget/top-10-funniest-text-messages-from-parents

[37] Yasseri T., Spoerri A., Graham M., and Kertész J., The most controversial topics in Wikipedia: A multilingual and geographical analysis. In: Fichman P., Hara N., editors, Global Wikipedia: International and cross-cultural issues in online collaboration. Scarecrow Press (2014).

[38] John Coleman, "Handwritten Notes Are a Rare Commodity. They're Also More Important Than Ever." *Harvard Business Review, April 5, 2013*, http://blogs.hbr.org/2013/04/handwritten-notes-are-a-rare-c/

[39] Stacy Miller, "You might save a life if you can stop the bullying," *Cumberland-Times News*, June 5, 2012, timesnews.com/opinion/ x916001996/You-might-save-a-life-if-you-can-stop-the-bullying

[40] K V Kurmanath, "Watch out for cyber bullies," *Business Line*, June 4, 2012, http://www.thehindubusinessline.com/features/eworld/article3489576. ece?ref=wl_features

[41] Samantha Murphy, "Rebecca Marino Quits Tennis Following Attacks on Social Media," *Mashable*, February 21, 2013, mashable.com/2013/02/21/ rebecca-marino-quits-tennis-social-media/

[42] "Bullied grandma in N.Y. bus video stunned by generosity," *CBC News*, June 22, 2012, http://www.cbc.ca/news/world/story/2012/06/21/ bullied-bus-monitor-karen-klein.html

[43] "Bullied grandma in N.Y. bus video stunned by generosity," *CBC News*, June 22, 2012, http://www.cbc.ca/news/world/story/2012/06/21/ bullied-bus-monitor-karen-klein.html

[44] Matt Bowen, "The real reason some brands outperform: authenticity. How you can do the same," *Aloft Group*, October 29, 2013, blog.aloft-group.com/aloft-group-insights-blog/the-real-reason-some-brands-outperform

[45] Mai Bruun Poulsen, "How a Rainbow-Oreo Sparked a Boycott and Doubled the Fan Growth," *Mndjumpers*, July 9, 2012, www.mindjumpers.com/blog/2012/07/oreo-boycott/

[46] Nick Wingfield, "A 'Black Box' on a Bike," *New York Times*, B1, July 21, 2012

[47] Claire Gordon, "Unemployed Hero Who Saved Baby Lands A Job," *AOL*, June 28, 2012, jobs.aol.com/articles/2012/06/28/unemployed-hero-who-saved-baby-lands-a-job/

[48] www.avg.com/press-releases-news & www.businesswire.com/news/ home/20101006006722/en/Digital-Birth-Online-World

[49] Chris Welch, "Michigan teen targeted in homecoming 'prank' gets last laugh" *CNN*, September 28, 2012, www.cnn.com/2012/09/28/us/ michigan-bullied-teen/index.html

[50] Crosbie, R. (2005). Learning the soft skills of leadership. Industrial and Commercial Training, 37(1), 45-51.

[51] "Cancer patient scores TD in Huskers spring game" *SI.com*, April 6, 2013 m.si.com/2693531/cancer-patient-scores-td-in-huskers-spring-game/

[52] Laken Litman, "Little Jack Hoffman an inspiration to Nebraska football" *USA Today*, April 9, 2013 www.usatoday.com/story/gameon/2013/ 04/08/jack-hoffman-cancer-patient-nebraska-spring-game/2065451/

?utm_source=feedburner&utm_medium=feed&utm_campaign=Feed%3
A+sportsmain+(Sports+-+Flipboard)

53 Judy Molland, "6 Girls Arrested For Facebook Attack-A-Teacher Day,"
Care 2 Make a Difference, January 08, 2011, www.care2.com/causes/
six-girls-arrested-for-facebook-attack-a-teacher-day.html

54 Howard Schultz, "Onward"

55 McKenzie Lock, "How Small Companies Can Beat the Big Guys and Win
Over the Top Talent," *LinkedIn Talent Blog,* October 17, 2013,
talent.linkedin.com/blog/index.php/2013/10/how-small-companies-
can-beat-the-big-guys-and-win-over-top-talent

56 Mark Gongloff, "Carl Icahn Tweet Boosts Apple's Stock Price By 3 Percent," *Huffington Post,* August 13, 2013, www.huffingtonpost.com/2013/
08/13/carl-icahn-apple-tweet_n_3750230.html

57 Todd Wassereman, "Twitter Being Used to Cast a Movie" *Mashable,*
February 7, 2013, mashable.com/2013/02/07/twitter-being-used-to-cast-
a-movie/

58 Kevin Joy and Amy Saunders, "Media frenzy overwhelms homeless man
with the 'golden voice,'" *The Columbus Dispatch,* January 6, 2011,
http://www.dispatch.com/content/stories/local/2011/01/06/
media-frenzy-overwhelms-columbus-golden-voice.html

59 Aylin Zafar, "Whatever Happened to Ted Williams, the 'Golden Voiced'
Homeless Man?" *Time,* January 13, 2012, newsfeed.time.com/2012/01/
13/whatever-happened-to-ted-williams-the-golden-voiced-homeless-man/

60 "Justin Bieber Net Worth," *The Richest,* http://www.therichest.org/
celebnetworth/celeb/singer/justin-bieber-net-worth/

61 Helen Kennedy, "Phoebe Prince, South Hadley High School's 'new girl,'
driven to suicide by teenage cyber bullies," *Daily News,* March 29, 2010,
http://www.nydailynews.com/news/national/phoebe-prince-south-
hadley-high-school-new-girl-driven-suicide-teenage-cyber-bullies-article-1
.165911

62 Robbie Owens, "Woman Barely Survives Texting & Driving Accident,"
CBS DFW, September 19, 2012, dfw.cbslocal.com/2012/09/19/woman-
barely-survives-texting-driving-accident/

63 Kevin Patra, "Wes Welker's wife sorry for ripping Ray Lewis," NFL,
January 22, 2013, http://www.nfl.com/news/story/
0ap1000000129520/printable/wes-welkers-wife-sorry-for-ripping-
ray-lewis

[64] "NYC bus driver Steven St. Bernard catches 7-year-old girl after 3-story fall," *CBS News*, July 17, 2012, http://www.cbsnews.com/8301-201_162-57473596/watch-nyc-bus-driver-steven-st-bernard-catches-7-year-old-girl-after-3-story-fall/

[65] Caleb Melby, "Billionaire T. Boone Pickens Sues His Son, Alleging 'Cyberbullying'" *Forbes*, April 16 2013, www.forbes.com/sites/caleb-melby/2013/04/16/billionaire-t-boone-pickens-sues-his-son-alleging-cyberbullying/

[66] "Explorations / Dervla Murphy," *British Airways High Life Magazine*, March, 2013

[67] Sharon Jayson, "Twitter could catch suicides early," *USA Today*, October 10, 2013, Section 3A

[68] Sharon Jayson, "Twitter could catch suicides early," *USA Today*, October 10, 2013, Section 3A

[69] Patrick Sawer, "Cyberbullying victims speak out: 'they were anonymous so they thought they could get away with it'," *The Telegraph*, November 13, 2011, http://www.telegraph.co.uk/technology/facebook/8885876/Cyber-bullying-victims-speak-out-they-were-anonymous-so-they-thought-they-could-get-away-with-it.html

[70] "Illinois College's Tucker wins college slam dunk contest" The State Journal-Register, April 1, 2011, www.sj-r.com/ sports/x910657607/ Illinois-Colleges-Tucker-wins-college-slam-dunk-contest

[71] Mark Schlabach, "NCAA Puts End to Jersey Sales," August 9, 2013, espn.go.com/college-sports/story/_/id/9551518/ ncaa-shuts-site-jersey-sales-says-hypocritical

[72] Post Staff Report, Eagles WR uses N-word in Angry Tirade at Kenny Chesney Concert," New York Post, July 31, 2013, nypost.com/2013/08/01/eagles-cooper-drops-the-n-word/

[73] Rick Chandler, "Young Ohio State Fan Who Named His Cancer 'Michigan' Invited to Wolverines' Game by Brady Hoke," Sports Grid, July 24, 2013, www.sportsgrid.com/ncaa-football/young-ohio-state-fan-who-named-his-cancer-michigan-invited-to-wolverines-game-by-brady-hoke/

[74] "Roddy White Reacts Harshly to George Zimmerman Verdict on Twitter," Huffington Post, July 14, 2013, www.huffingtonpost.com/2013/07/14/ roddy-white-george-zimmerman-verdict-twitter_n_3593212.html

[75] "Lee Westwood Apologizes for Tweets," *ESPN*, August 12, 2013, http://espn.go.com/golf/pgachampionship13/story/_/id/9559921/ lee-westwood-sorry-twitter-rant-ian-poulter-let-team-next?

[76] Donna Leinwand Leger, "End of the road for 'Silk Road,' *USA Today*, October 3, 2013, Section A1

[77] Andrew Mach, "Massachusetts teen sentenced to prison for texting while driving," *NBC News*, June 6, 2012, usnews.nbcnews.com/_news/2012/06/06/12090348-massachusetts-teen-sentenced-to-prison-for-texting-while-driving?lite

[78] Richard Wolf, "Can your cellphone data be used against you?," *USA Today*, September 10, 2013 Section 1A

[79] John Bacon, "Man indicted after YouTube confession," *USA Today*, September 10, 2013 Section 2A

[80] Beth Greenfield, "Dumbest Facebook Post Ever?," *Shine*, January 5, 2013, shine.yahoo.com/healthy-living/dumbest-facebook-post-ever-170100535.html

[81] "Joseph Bernard Campbell Stole Nude Photos And Posted Them On Victims' Facebook Pages," *Huffington Post*, July 22, 20111, http://www.huffingtonpost.com/2011/07/22/joseph-bernard-campbell-stole-nude-photos_n_906975.html

[82] Matt Chorley, "Police grapple with internet troll epidemic as convictions for posting online abuse soar by 150% in just four years," *MailOnline*, November 15, 2012, www.dailymail.co.uk/news/article-2233428/Police-grapple-internet-troll-epidemic-convictions-posting-online-abuse-soar-150-cent-just-years.html

[83] American Red Cross, "Mission, Vision, and Fundamental Principles, www.redcross.org/about-us/mission

MUST-READS

Delivering Happiness by Tony Hsieh
Made to Stick & Switch by Dan & Chip Heath
Uncommon & Quiet Strength by Tony Dungy
and Nathan Whitaker
7 Habits of Highly Effective People by Stephen Convey
True North by Bill George
How to Win Friends and Influence People by Dale Carnegie
Stop Worrying and Start Living by Dale Carnegie
Platform by Michael Hyatt
Good to Great by Jim Collins
Now Discover Your Strengths by Marcus Buckingham
Inbound Marketing by Brian Halligan & Dharmesh Shah
The New Rules of Marketing and PR by David Meerman Scott
Likeable and *Likeable Leadership* by David Kerpen
Onward by Howard Schultz
Enchantment by Guy Kawasaki
The Facebook Effect by David Kirkpatrick
Groundswell by Charlene Li and Josh Bernoff
The Social Media Bible by Lon Safko
Unbroken by Laura Hildebrandt
The Lean Start-Up by Eric Reis
Inbound Marketing by Brian Halligan and Dharmesh Shah
Shark Tank Jump Start Your Business by Michael Parrish DuDell

ACKNOWLEDGEMENTS

They say it takes a small village to raise a child. Well, it takes a big village to publish a book. I'm fortunate to be surrounded by the most talented village in the world. I can't thank everyone enough!

- **FAMILY:** Your names should always be on the cover, starting with my beautiful and talented wife/mother Ana Maria. Sofia Brook, Katia, Mom, Dad, Grandma, Granddad, Abuelo, Lolis, Jay, Matt, Helene, Mary Alison, Jose, Stephanie, Cesar. You all mean the world to me.

- **COURTNEY O'CONNELL:** You have a finished book in your hands because Courtney figured out everything from printing to proofreading. Incredible.

- **JOAN KATZ:** Amazing editor.

- **DAN DINSMORE:** Incredible cover design

- **EMILY ZARA, EMILY HOEKSEMA, SARAH YORK:** Incredible research, marketing, research and design. Even better attitudes!

- **TOM DEVER, TAMARA DEVER, ERIN STARK, AND MONICA THOMAS OF TLC GRAPHICS:** The book doctors and interior and exterior book design gurus.

- **JASON ILLIAN:** CEO of BookShout, Christian, author and digital publishing expert.

Influencers:

Thanks for always being generous with your time, insights and personal advice:

Tony Hsieh, Magic Johnson, Guy Kawasaki, Scott Monty, Tom Izzo, Chris Brogan, David Kerpen, Mark Hollis, Angelo Pizzo, Angel Martinez, C.C. Chapman, Mike Lewis, Ann Handley, Jeremiah Owyang, David Berkowitch, Alex Hult, Eddie Hult, Hakan Sjoo, Brian Solis, Phyllis Kare, Andrea Vahl, Gary Vaynerchuk, Chris Loughlin, Sean Cook, Mari Smith, Michael Stelzner, David Meerman Scott, John Hill, Mark Hollis, Lon Safko, Philip Hult, Josh Linkner, Dan Zarella, Jim Keppler, Gary McManis, Paul Gillan, Mike Volpe, Dean Gilligan, Ralph Bartel, Lutz Bethge, Bill Hallock, Brian Reich, Gary and Michael Lewis.

Friends & Supporters:

A book like this doesn't happen without great supporters like these:

Mark Oldemeyer, Jim Darling, Scott Mueller, Scott Tynes, Bill Klein, Steve Amoia, Kim Klein, Anthony, Dave Banas, Jennifer Barrett, Sybril Bennett, Jason Bhatti, Satyen Bhujun, Ron Blackmore, Dale Blasingame, Renee' Bovair, Wayne Breitbarth, Cortney Brewer, Piers Brown, Stephanie Engels, Bobbie Carlton, Brendan Casey, Mark Engels, Jason Caston, Chandler, Dorie Clark, Marc Colando, Sean Cook, Ludwina Dautovic, Ben Davis, Kathleen Welsh, Marlene De Quesada, Denise DeSimone, Perry Drake, Scott Dubois, Linda Duffy, Kevin Mueller, Mark Engels, Derek Fasi, Martha Fernandez, Jill Ford, Wayne Fredin, Rob Friedman, Scott Galloway, Christie Germans, Sandy Mueller, Anthony Gill, Paul Goldenberg,

Susan R Grossman, Peter Hendrick, Ty Hooge, David Jenyns, Bernhard Jodeleit, Mark A Johnson, Doug Johnston, JP Kane, Ann Handley, Kamron Karington, Gumundur Karl Karlsson, Alexander Kassab, Carol Katz, Dave Kerpen, Reiner Mueller, Phyllis Khare, Philip Kiger, Josh Kohnert, Nancy Kohutek, Danica Kombol, Sagar Lakhani, James E. Lee, Matt Levin, Peter Linder, Lindsey, Rafaela Lotto, Jen Low, Leonardo Magalhaes, Janine McBee, Tom McCallum, April McCormack, Tim McDonald, Matt McHale, Mike D. Merrill, Cesar Molano, Nikki Baize Moran, Arnobio Morelix, Fraser Motion, Kevin O'Connell, , Kathleen Parente, Lisa Wiley Parker, Chris Perkins, Lars Perner, Steve Polonowski, Dustin Ramsdell, Sam Ramus, David Redelberger, Brian Reich, Eddy Ricci, Jason Rubley, Mike Saunders, Joe Schwartz, Stephen Selby, Howard Silverstone, Welmoed Sisson, Patrick Sitkins, Jordan Skole, Shane Snow, Lisa Tener, Ingolfur Thorsteinsson, Rockhopper Ventures, Vikram, Diane Walter, Richard Ware, Tim Washer, Jess Wearn, Colin Whaley, Warren Whitlock, Lizzie Williams, Todd Wiseley.

IN OUR PRAYERS: Ron Jones

ABOUT ERIK QUALMAN

Often called a Digital Dale Carnegie, Erik Qualman is the author of *Socialnomics: How Social Media Transforms the Way We Live and Do Business*. Socialnomics made Amazon's #1 Best Selling List for the US, Japan, UK, Canada, Portugal, Italy, China, Korea and Germany. His book *Digital Leader* propelled him to be voted the 2nd Most Likeable Author in the World behind Harry Potter's J.K. Rowling.

His work has been featured on 60 Minutes to the Wall Street Journal and used by the National Guard to NASA. He recently gave the commencement address at the University of Texas and has spoken in 42 countries for the likes of Coach, Sony, IBM, Facebook, Starbucks, Chase, M&M/Mars, Cartier, Montblanc, TEDx, Polo, UGG, Nokia, Google and many more.

Socialnomics was a finalist for the "Book of the Year." Qualman wrote and produced the world's most watched social media video "Social Media Revolution." In his past, Qualman was Academic All-Big Ten in basketball at Michigan State University and in 2011, Erik was honored as the *Michigan State University Alum of the Year*. He also has an MBA from the McCombs School of Business.

Additional Books & Resources by Erik Qualman

Socialnomics: How Social Media Transforms the Way We Live and Do Business

**Order here:
bit.ly/socialnomics-book2**

Digital Leader: How Digital Leaders are Made—Not Born. The 5 Simple Keys to Success in the Digital Era

**Order here:
amzn.to/leader-kindle**

www.equalman.com

www.socialnomics.com